MR. ALL-AROUND

MR. ALL-AROUND

THE LIFE OF

Tom Gola

DAVID GRZYBOWSKI

Foreword by BILL RAFTERY

TEMPLE UNIVERSITY PRESS   *Philadelphia • Rome • Tokyo*

TEMPLE UNIVERSITY PRESS
Philadelphia, Pennsylvania 19122
tupress.temple.edu

Design by Kate Nichols

Library of Congress Cataloging-in-Publication Data

Names: Grzybowski, David, 1991– author.
Title: Mr. All-Around : the life of Tom Gola / David Grzybowski ; with
    a foreword by Bill Raftery.
Description: Philadelphia : Temple University Press, 2018. | Includes
    bibliographical references and index. |
Identifiers: LCCN 2018018511 (print) | LCCN 2018027501 (ebook) |
    ISBN 9781439916810 (E-book) | ISBN 9781439916797 (cloth : alk. paper)
Subjects: LCSH: Gola, Tom, 1933–2014. | Basketball players—United
    States—Biography. | Basketball coaches—United States—Biography. |
    Politicians—Pennsylvania—Biography.
Classification: LCC GV884.G65 (ebook) | LCC GV884.G65 G79 2018 (print) |
    DDC 796.323092 [B]—dc23
LC record available at https://lccn.loc.gov/2018018511

Printed in the United States of America

9 8 7 6 5 4 3 2 1

. . . .

To my wife, Jodi;

the Grzybowski family;

Caroline and the Gola family;

Brother Joseph Grabenstein, FSC;

and La Salle Explorers

everywhere

. . . .

Contents

Photographs follow page 72

Foreword

IFIRST MET TOM GOLA when I was a high school senior while attending a New York Knicks basketball game at the old Madison Square Garden, on 7th Avenue between 49th and 50th Streets. I was escorted into the Knicks locker room to be introduced to Tom at the end of a rough-and-tough National Basketball Association (NBA) game.

As a youngster, I had read and heard of Tom's extraordinary exploits during his days at La Salle College. I was in awe of his many amazing accomplishments as a player. His Explorer teams were an important fixture on the national basketball landscape. Anyone who played the game knew of his Most Valuable Player (MVP) role in the 1952 National Invitation Tournament (NIT) championship and his Player of the Year honors and National Collegiate Athletic Association (NCAA) championships in 1954. They also knew of his team's NCAA loss in 1955 to Bill Russell and the Dons of San Francisco.

Standing in front of him in the Garden that day, I could tell that his success was unimportant to him. He was so at ease with himself that I became totally relaxed in his presence. He showed interest in me and my future. La Salle's help in maturing him as a student had prepared him for what would come in the next fifty years of his life.

In reflecting on that evening with Tom, I recall that I was then—as I would be throughout his life—impressed with his humility. He never talked about himself or his incredible contributions to La Salle or the NBA. His down-to-earth demeanor was one of the major influences on my decision to attend La Salle. At various times since our initial meeting, I had the opportunity to visit with him. His approach to life, family, school, and friends remained unchanged.

One story I was told illustrates his unswerving priorities and view of life. Tom respectfully declined a White House invitation from President Richard Nixon, not out of any disdain for the president but because he had a particularly important prior commitment: he had invited his dad to go to the Jersey Shore for a day of fishing in Wildwood. This story is only one of many that reflect Tom's remarkable perspective on life.

As the years progressed, I saw Tom infrequently, but two visits with him were memorable for his marvelous sense of humor. Bill Cunningham and I called on him after his first stroke, when he was facing rehab. He was lamenting his weight loss and his thinning legs. I responded that his legs looked fine and that they were still more robust than mine. "Please," he said, referring to my legs, "I would really look in bad shape if my legs looked as thin as those."

The second visit was a trip to La Salle for a meet and greet with former head basketball coach John Giannini. Tom and I were both on the elevator when he looked at me and said playfully, "Your hair is gray." Knowing that I had been gray since my early twenties, everyone on the elevator broke into laughter. Tom displayed charm and grace throughout his lifetime.

David Grzybowski has captured Tom's story and the richness of his character. Chronicling his success as a player, coach, politician, husband, and dad, he reveals Tom's full depth. La Salle University graduates will be delighted that this book presents to the public not only Tom's many career contributions but also his innate goodness.

—Bill Raftery
Broadcaster

MR. ALL-AROUND

Introduction

*Today, I am a contented person. I gave it my best
in all that I did, in sports businesses and in public office.
I would have never second-guessed myself.*

—TOM GOLA

"HISTORY STANDS on the legacies of others."
That's what La Salle University's archivist, Brother Joe Grabenstein, told me during my senior year at La Salle in 2013.

With the help of Brother Joe, I had the exclusive opportunity to interview Tom Gola in February 2013, a month before the Atlantic 10 Tournament in Brooklyn, New York. This request to interview the La Salle legend was unheard of from a member of the student body. No one from the university had heard from Gola in years, as he quietly recovered from a fall back in 2003.

It was a cold Sunday afternoon when I interviewed him. He was parked at his usual spot in a hallway at St. Joseph's Manor, a long-term-care facility not ten miles north from where the basketball star had grown up, reading his morning paper. His size 15 shoes rested comfortably on his wheelchair.

Although a stroke made it difficult for Gola to speak, he had no problem identifying the origins of his storied college basketball career at La Salle and, later, a successful run in the National Basketball Association (NBA), coaching, and politics.

"I was born with these hands," Gola explained. "They were given to me by God."

When March Madness kicked off in 2013, the La Salle Explorers had earned a spot in the National Collegiate Athletic Association (NCAA) tournament for the first time since 1992. They then beat Boise State, Kansas State, and Ole Miss to advance to the Sweet 16 for the first time since 1955, when Gola's old team had made its run. As La Salle advanced in the tournament, the history of the 1954 national championship team and Gola's legacy regained interest.

This book was conceived on November 21, when I decided that Tom Gola's full story needed to be told. Ironically, the city of Philadelphia designated November 21 as "Tom Gola Day" back in 1998, in recognition of the dedication of a new basketball arena in his name.

That building, Tom Gola Arena, was officially dedicated three months later on La Salle's campus—on February 21, my birthday. People speak of basketball gods who make sure the ball bounces just right to keep basketball history on track for its fated moments. The La Salle basketball gods were telling me something.

. . . .

ON JANUARY 13, 1933, the future icon of La Salle basketball was born to Ike Gola, a police officer, and his wife, Helen, in a small row home in the Olney section of Philadelphia, Pennsylvania, near the corner of 3rd and Lindley. The Golas raised their seven children in the small, close-knit, blue-collar Incarnation Parish community.

Through mentors and teachers at Incarnation, young Tom Gola learned the game of basketball. His physique and on-court prowess blossomed in grade school, filling up stat sheets throughout the city. Gola was recruited heavily by La Salle College High School, where he played under the legendary coach Charles "Obie" O'Brien. His mother wanted him to remain close to the Christian Brothers, the Catholic educational tradition followed at Incarnation, so Gola stayed in Philadelphia to attend La Salle College in 1951.

Gola's college career on the campus at 20th and Olney kicked off with a freshman year win in the National Invitation Tournament (NIT) championship at Madison Square Garden under La Salle coach Ken Loeffler. Over the next three years, Gola racked up achievements and accolades, including the NCAA championship in 1954, the Helms Foundation College Basketball Player of the Year Award, three All-American distinctions, and a matchup against Bill Russell and the San Francisco Dons in the 1955 NCAA championship. Gola also inked his name into the record books, scoring more than 2,000 points and setting the still-unbroken NCAA Division I rebounding record, grabbing 2,201.

Gola did not have to travel far to begin his professional NBA career, being drafted by the Philadelphia Warriors in 1956. During his rookie season, Gola contributed to the franchise's first NBA championship as a starting shooting guard. Uncle Sam came calling the next year, and Gola joined the ranks of the U.S. Army, with which he traveled up and down the East Coast, working in a cryptography school and coding at the Army Signal School.

After serving his country, Gola resumed his professional basketball career with the Philadelphia Warriors in the 1957–1958 season. When the Warriors franchise moved to San Francisco, California, Gola followed the team, but his heart was still in Philadelphia. After a brief stint out west, Gola was traded to the New York Knicks, where he finished his ten-season career in the NBA in 1966. To this day, Gola is only one of two players to win the NIT, NCAA, and NBA championships. One of his most prized accomplishments was playing on the "Behind the Iron Curtain Tour" in 1964, a European trip promoting American basketball with such NBA legends as Bill Russell, Tom Heinsohn, K.C. Jones, Oscar Robertson, Jerry Lucas, Bob Pettit, and Bob Cousy.

Gola traded in his jersey and shorts for a suit and tie when he served as a member of Pennsylvania House of Representatives for the 170th district in Philadelphia from 1967 to 1968, prior to coaching at La Salle. Gola later became the Philadelphia city controller from 1970 to 1974, joining the politician Arlen Specter on a joint campaign that revolutionized political marketing within Philadelphia.

Determined to help revamp its damaged basketball program, Gola became La Salle College's basketball coach in 1968. To many college basketball fans' estimation, Gola coached one of the best Big 5 basketball teams in Philadelphia history, leading a 23–1 team featuring such players as Ken Durrett, Larry Cannon, Roland Taylor, and Fran Dunphy. After leaving the coaching seat in 1970, Gola made a brief run at the Philadelphia mayor's office in 1983, losing in the Republican primary.

Gola continued to be a staple in Philadelphia through his commitment to public service, sports, and the La Salle community until his death on January 26, 2014.

Throughout Gola's life, he remained loyal to his family, teammates, political acquaintances, and fans. As a proud La Salle University alum and a passionate basketball fan, I believe that my legacy is to tell Gola's story.

Note: Unattributed quotations are from interviews I conducted while researching this book.

1

....

3rd and Lindley

TOM GOLA WAS INTRODUCED to the game of basketball during the summer of 1944, when he was about to enter the sixth grade at Incarnation Grammar School in Philadelphia. Father Joseph Belz, a pastor at the church, formed a school basketball team and entered the kids in the Catholic Youth Organization league. The school's gym was located in the basement of 5th and Lindley, which had a low ceiling, two basketball nets, a bowling alley, card tables, pool tables, a television room, and concession stands to accommodate students and members of the Olney neighborhood.

The man in charge of it all was the club manager, coach, and neighborhood mentor Lefty Huber. Huber was the mother hen of the community and the athletic director of the Incarnation Catholic Club, which put him in charge of all gym activities. Father Belz got the wheels in motion for the Incarnation kids to have an opportunity to play ball, but "it was Lefty Huber who was the big influence on Tommy," says Claire Gola, Tom's younger sister.

Gola met Huber as a 13-year-old entering the seventh grade at Incarnation. Gola, who was already close to 5 ft. 7 in., was too tall not to play basketball. Gola, who also served as an altar boy for the parish, recalled picking the number 15 for his Incarnation jersey: "That was the only number I could get," he said. "I took the number 15 when that was left to me."

The Golas recall that Huber would come to their house and practice with Tom under a homemade basketball net made by his father, Isadore (nicknamed Izzy or Ike). The net, which was located next to the Golas' chicken coop, was made from wire attached to a wooden backboard.

"It gave you a chance to wax on your game, as they say," says John Gola, Tom's younger brother.

These one-on-one practices were not daily occurrences, but Huber paid a lot of attention to Gola. At times, he took kids from Incarnation, including Gola, to see the Philadelphia Warriors play.

"Lefty Huber used to take us to see the 1947 Philadelphia Warriors. That was the start of the NBA," Gola said.

Gola patterned his game after that of the Philadelphia Warrior Howie Dallmar, a University of Pennsylvania graduate from San Francisco, California. Dallmar played with the Philadelphia Warriors in the Basketball Association of America (BAA) from 1946 to 1949 and was known for his gliding jump shot and his underhand lay-up.

When he was in the eighth grade, Gola had the height and size but needed agility and speed to take his game to the next level. Huber wanted to change Gola into a pivot basketball player, which would let him move around the paint, call for the ball, facilitate plays for his team, and become a better scorer. Some of Huber's practice drills consisted of Gola and his teammates lining up chairs on the court and weaving in and out of them while dribbling at top speed. Huber sometimes waved a dollar bill in the faces of his players to bet against their own odds on the free throw line. The basketball court at Incarnation, with its old, low ceiling, was not ideal. The facility's cramped conditions forced the school's players to learn to shoot on an angle or with a line drive shot to the basket.

"That ceiling was tough. That's why Tommy's shot was like a line drive. From what I understand, Tommy did not have an arc on his shoot because of the club," says Dennis Fiandra, a 1959 graduate of Incarnation and Olney native. "We had that low ceiling, [and] it was tough to play down there for another team. The court was small and all."

Gola's basketball IQ began to blossom, and his work on the court started getting noticed around Philadelphia. During his last season at Incarnation, as an eighth grader, Gola scored 816 points, helping his team win more than thirty games in a row.

During Gola's last year at Incarnation, members of the Incarnation

Parish and former school basketball players hosted a testimonial dinner to donate money to Huber for his years of service to the parish, the school, and the community. He graciously declined the money, instead earmarking the funds for student athletes deserving of scholarships to La Salle College High School.

The Gola family breadwinner was Tom's father, Isadore Gola, or "Izzy" for short. (Some family members also called him "Ike.") Izzy worked as a police officer in the city of Philadelphia, patrolling 19th and Buttonwood Streets.

Izzy frequently worked various shifts throughout the week—five days on one shift, five days on another, switching week after week until the end of the month. Although being a police officer was his main job, he also worked as a mechanic for the Yellow Cab Company on the side.

"He was such a good mechanic [that] they let him make his own hours," says Paul Gola, Tom's younger brother (called "Mo" by the Gola family).

Tom Gola had six brothers and sisters: Wanda, Joan, John, Catherine, Paul, and Claire. Tom was the third child, born after Wanda and Joan. Izzy came home from his long shifts on the police force and went straight to work as a mechanic, even if the shift was for a mere two or three hours, to complete his sixteen-hour work days. Everyone in the Gola family knew that Izzy was a handyman, to say the least; Paul recalls a time when John got into a car accident and their father fixed the entire car in their backyard, installing two fenders, a brand-new hood, and a brand-new motor.

Izzy worked tireless hours, wanting to give his family a better life than he had had. Consequently, Tom and his siblings rarely saw their father. John recalls that when any one of his brothers or sisters came home at night, their mother would put a finger up to her mouth, saying, "Daddy is sleeping." Not having their father around was something the Golas sometimes had to explain to family and friends.

"I saw my dad on Christmas, Thanksgiving, Easter, and two weeks in Wildwood," laughs John Gola, Tom's brother. "That's when I saw him."

"You never knew when he was going to be home or when he wasn't going to be home. It was different. My mother was the ruler of the house," says Joan Gola, Tom's sister. "My father was a man who didn't have much to say. My father was very quiet."

For Izzy, working as a police officer and a mechanic was a necessity, as Tom's mother, Helen Milecki Gola, did not work. Helen was born in the

United States but later went back to her extended family in Poland; she returned to the United States years later. Neither of Tom's parents attended high school, but Helen stayed true to her heritage and taught her kids to speak Polish. John even remembers reciting the "Our Father" entirely in Polish.

"My mother was the leader in the house," recalls Joan.

Helen was the family homemaker and unofficial Polish cook. When the Golas sat down in their small kitchen, *galumpkis* (stuffed cabbage), steaks, lasagna, dumplings, and other Polish dishes dressed the table. She frequently bought steaks at a 5th Street market to cook the family's morning favorite of steak and eggs, but her favorite meal to prepare was Polish pierogi, especially on one of her favorite holidays, Christmas Eve. Helen and sometimes Claire would make pierogi a week before Christmas, freeze them, and serve them at 6:00 P.M. on Christmas Eve.

The Golas lived at 5110 Lindley Avenue, a row home in the Olney section of North Philadelphia. The children had to share rooms growing up, with three boys—Tom, John, and Paul—all sharing one room. The two oldest boys, Tom and John, shared one king-size bed, while Paul's bed was a fold-up mattress closest to the door. Tom and John frequently had to climb over the sleeping Paul to get to their bed.

The intersection at 3rd and Lindley was busy in the 1950s, with businesses on each corner across and to the side of the Golas' house. On one corner was Sie Rubenstein's, a candy store owned and operated by a local Jewish family. The candy shop was the kids' go-to spot for Milky Ways, penny candies, and licorice—both red and black flavors—as well as sodas, ice cream, and milkshakes. On the other corner was a German bakery called Beutel. The Golas' home was within walking distance of the A. J. Morrison Elementary School.

"It was nice growing up on that street," says Claire.

The children in the Olney community played basketball, street hockey, and half ball, a sport played with a broomstick and half of a pimple ball. The neighborhood was a tight-knit community made up of Irish and Italian families. There was always something to do, and if any of the children acted out of line in anyway, their families would find out. In those days, all the families knew each other.

Tom was a good influence. "If it wasn't for [Tom], there would have been a lot of men from Olney who would probably be wearing stripes and numbers," says Frank Dailey, a 1948 graduate of Incarnation.

Mary Mielewska (or "Bushi," depending on whom you spoke to) was the Gola children's grandmother. Bushi lived with the Golas for an extended period. She originally came over from Poland with her three girls and husband.

"She was a tall lady—I know that. My mother used to always tell me that she could stand in the back of the church and see over everybody's head," says Joan Gola.

Bushi passed away from cancer when Joan was in the fifth grade. Joan became Helen's assistant cook.

The Golas' annual family vacation in Wildwood, New Jersey, started on the last day of school and ended on the last day of summer. They would make the hundred-mile haul "down the shore" to rent a house for the three months of summer. John recalls that the trips to Wildwood almost didn't happen, as Izzy had to borrow money—anywhere from $600 to $1,600—from his brother-in-law just to put the deposit on the house. Izzy made the trip down to Wildwood on the days he had off, but he primarily stayed in Philadelphia to continue working with the Yellow Cab Company and the police department.

Being "down the shore" all summer was not all fun and games for the Gola children. All of them had to help find a little source of income for the summer. Tom and his brother John worked as lifeguards and in the kitchen at Zaberer's, a restaurant in the Anglesea section of North Wildwood. John recalls making close to $35 a week, with Uncle Sam taking $8 and his mother taking $25, leaving him with the rest for his own personal spending. Paul worked on the beach as well, setting up beach chairs and umbrellas for people spending their day by the ocean, while their sister Joan was a waitress at Holidays, a restaurant on the Wildwood boardwalk.

The hot attraction in Wildwood for Tom and his brothers was not the boardwalk. Instead, it was Larry Kenney's house, located at 26th and Central in North Wildwood, where the locals played basketball. "Old Man Kenney," as some called him back in the day, was a casket maker from Philadelphia with a large home that included several garages and a basketball court. Kenney played basketball at one point for the St. Joseph's Hawks and was known for having fancy cars and a giant freezer for ice cream in his garage.

"It was the spot to be in the summer time. We would play ball all morning, and then we would go and do our jobs in the afternoon," says John. "It was great. It was a lot of good times."

Kenney's house was located just two blocks away from the beach. The Golas, primarily Tom and John, sometimes worked from early morning to mid-afternoon, went back to their house to put their bathing suits on, and then played basketball for an hour or two. After basketball was finished, the gang headed down to the beach, went back home to shower, and then continued to play basketball into the night. The games at Kenney's house included, at times, an all-star cast, with appearances from NBA greats Bob Cousy and Paul Arizin.

Tom Gola graduated from Incarnation Grammar School in 1948. His next stop: La Salle College High School in Philadelphia.

2

· · · · · · · ·

La Salle College
High School

AS REMAINS THE CASE in Philadelphia high school basketball, in 1948, a player with Tom Gola's physical and mental advantages was highly sought after. Gola stood 5 ft. 9 in. heading into high school and would grow 2 more inches in his freshman year alone.

"He was the best in the city at the time," says Paul "Mo" Gola, Tom's younger brother. "La Salle wanted him. If he didn't want to go to La Salle, he would have ended up at North Catholic."

La Salle College High School was—and is—more familiarly known as La Salle High. During Gola's years at the school, La Salle High occupied its own large building on the La Salle College campus at 20th Street and Olney Avenue in Philadelphia. In 1960, La Salle High moved to its current campus in Wyndmoor, Pennsylvania.

During Gola's early high school years, in addition to playing basketball, he ran track (he broke the Catholic high school record in the half mile) and played football and baseball. La Salle's head basketball coach, Charles "Obie" O'Brien, wanted to prevent any injuries to Gola, so Gola quit playing football at O'Brien's request early in his high school career. Even though Gola didn't see a lot of action on the hardwood until his sophomore year, he had a taste of what it was like to win and understood what it took to be successful at La Salle High.

Gola told the *Philadelphia Inquirer* in 1978, "Obie O'Brien has helped thousands of kids by teaching them good fundamental basketball. He has the ability to instill in the individual a quality which he describes in a word . . . 'moxie.' I feel that every boy who had the personal coaching of Obie O'Brien can consider himself very fortunate."

O'Brien's love for the game of basketball started while he was growing up on the streets of Kensington in Northeast Philadelphia. He attended West Catholic High School, where he won All-Catholic and All-Scholastic honors playing basketball. After attending West Catholic, O'Brien's basketball career continued at Temple University. After graduating from Temple, O'Brien became the head basketball coach at La Salle High in 1934. He started the swimming program in 1936 and coached the track team for twenty-one years. In 1942, O'Brien left La Salle High to become the head basketball coach at La Salle College, where he coached for three seasons with a 33–29 record. O'Brien then returned to La Salle High to serve as head coach in 1944. O'Brien coached for thirty-four straight years at La Salle High, earning a 541–248 record.

Gola started his high school career playing on La Salle's bench behind such players as John Grauer, Jim Covello, Charles "Buddy" Donnelly, Tom Checchia, and Dan Kane. The "Little Explorers," as La Salle's team was called, won the Catholic League title at the Palestra, defeating Philadelphia native Ernie Beck and his West Catholic Burrs. Beck graduated and then played basketball at the University of Pennsylvania; he was drafted by the Philadelphia Warriors in 1953. Beck went on to play in the National Basketball Association (NBA) for the Hawks and the Nationals. The Little Explorers followed that victory with a 39–38 win over Overbrook High School in the city championship game, in which Donnelly made the game-winning shot. He later starred at La Salle College.

In 1949, Gola's sophomore year, La Salle High lost in the semifinals, 41–33, to a West Catholic team coached by Joe Langan. West Catholic had a 19–7 record that season, thanks to a team led by Ernie Beck, Ed Garrity, Tom Holt, Ned Hogan, Tom McCormick, and Jack Devine. Beck received All-Catholic Honors in 1948 and 1949 and was presented with the Markward Award, named after the former Roman Catholic High School coach William Markward and given each year to the most valuable high school basketball players from the Public and the Catholic League teams.

In 1950, Gola's junior season, La Salle High beat West Catholic, 54–40, in the semifinals of the Catholic League playoffs, a game in which Gola netted 22 points and teammate Frank "Wacky" O'Hara scored 13. La Salle later beat South Catholic High School, 28–23, at the Palestra in the Catholic League title game. The championship game was the lowest-scoring play-off game in Catholic League history due to poor ball handling and shooting from the Explorers and the South Catholic Pirates. Gola was named to the 1950 All-Catholic team, which included O'Hara as well.

Gola continued his winning ways in the City Championship game, where he scored 20 points in a 55–31 rout of Overbrook. In contrast to the Catholic League championship game, the final score was the highest team total in a city title play-off game and the largest margin of victory since the 1939 City Championship game. Gola received the Markward Award for having led La Salle to its third city title in five years, making him the first La Salle High player to win the award.

Gola's best season at La Salle High was his senior year, in 1951. He averaged 25.6 points per game and scored 333 points during the 13 regular season games. La Salle's season was cut short in 1951, when the team lost to St. Thomas More in the Catholic League semifinals; Gola was held to 14 points in this loss. Despite not reaching the Catholic League Finals, Gola won the Markward Award for the second straight year, completing his decorated high school career.

O'Brien told the *Philadelphia Bulletin* in 1955, "There is no doubt Gola is the best all-around player I ever coached. He never gave me a minute of trouble and was always ready to learn. Tom has perfect temperament for an athlete. He is humble and loyal. What coach could ask for more?"

After the season ended, Gola was selected to play in the national North versus South All-Star high school game at Murray State College (now Murray State University) in Murray, Kentucky. The game also included all-stars Ned Clark, Alva Winfred "Win" Wilfong, Charles Mencel, and Dean Parsons. Charles "Chuck" Taylor, the owner of the Converse shoe company, was involved with the all-star game committee and game presentations. The North team defeated the South team, 83–70, and Gola scored 10 points.

Gola's accolades kept coming as the spring wore on. During the awards season, Gola became friends with Benjamin Franklin High School player

John Chaney, who would be the head basketball coach at Temple University from 1982 to 2006.

After the 1951 season, the Catholic and the Public Leagues held their seasons' joint sports banquet at the Warwick Hotel on South 17th Street in Center City, Philadelphia. The ceremony was to highlight and honor the past season's teams and players and to hand out the Markward Awards. The banquet's dress code was black-tie, so attendees were expected to wear a suit. For Chaney, dress clothes were hard to come by.

"I never had a suit," says Chaney.

Chaney ended up wearing one of his stepfather's suits with wide lapels, a big tie hanging over his belt, and padded shoulders. Chaney felt embarrassed about the way he looked.

"As soon as I got there, I started to hide out places," he says.

Chaney walked into the Warwick Hotel and straight to the men's restroom, where he stood on the toilet seat so no one could see his feet. As the night went on, other players looked for Chaney. At one point, Gola came into the restroom looking for Chaney, as the photographer was going to take photos of the award winners.

"Johnny, you in here? Come on out. We are going to take pictures," Chaney recalls Gola saying.

Gola escorted him out of the restroom to take photos as they received their Public and Catholic League trophies.

Chaney and Gola's relationship grew over the years, and they always stayed in touch during Chaney's long coaching stint with Temple University. Chaney recalls seeing the development of Gola's game during his time at La Salle High.

"What was unique about him was something no one has ever mentioned: that fact that he was an excellent defensive player. One of the great qualities he had while playing defense," Chaney said. "He invented this. . . . If he was playing defense on you and you went around him, he would do this wrap-around and tap the ball away and take off. He even did that in the pros."

That mix of aggressive offense and stingy defense had colleges and universities jumping to show Gola how much they wanted him to play for their schools. College recruiters flocked to games and even practices throughout the final months of the basketball season. Newspapers reported that Gola received between fifty-seven and eighty scholarship offers. However, Gola's brother, Paul, thinks the number was somewhere near one hundred fifty.

"It was hard for Tom to choose a school because there was a lot of good schools after him," Paul says.

Gola received local recognition from the likes of the University of Pennsylvania, Temple University, and La Salle. Larger institutions, including Notre Dame, Duquesne, St. Louis, Oklahoma A&M, Navy, Georgetown, Syracuse, Manhattan, Kentucky, and North Carolina State, also pursued Gola's talents. With little to no television exposure, recruiting was difficult for some college teams trying to entice potential players to head to another state. During his senior year's Easter break, Gola and O'Brien went on a college tour to visit Notre Dame, Kentucky, Duke, and North Carolina State. Mo remembers that Everett Case, North Carolina State's basketball coach from 1946 to 1964, made the 417-mile trip from Raleigh, North Carolina, to Philadelphia to meet the Gola family in person.

"What would you like for your son, Mr. Gola?" Mo recalls Case asking.

Gola's father did not want to take side money for his son's basketball services, even though the offer appeared to be close to $250 a month for joining North Carolina State. This financial gesture was not a scholarship but an added bonus to incentivize Gola to head down to Raleigh.

"If Tom went to Kentucky or North Carolina State, he would just be another All-American. That really wasn't his goal in life, to go down south to play ball and get those accomplishments," says John Gola.

Gola narrowed his choices to North Carolina State and La Salle College.

"Actually I [had] pretty much decided on North Carolina State," Gola told *La Salle Magazine* in 1994. "I made one trip with my father, then another with Obie [Charles O'Brien], but each time the offer was different. I began to say to myself, what's going on here?"

The uncertainty and mixed signals soured O'Brien and Gola on the prospect of Gola's going south for college. O'Brien believed that it was in Gola's best interests to stay true to his roots in Philadelphia and attend La Salle.

Gola's mother, Helen, was very partial to the Christian Brothers and had a great influence on her son's college decision. She wanted to see her son play basketball, but she didn't want to travel to do so. La Salle College's head coach, Ken Loeffler, kept a close eye on Gola but didn't introduce himself until Gola graduated.

"I had never met Kenny Loeffler," Gola told *La Salle Magazine* in 1994. "The man who actually recruited me was Brother Stanislaus."

In the spring of 1951, Brother Erminus Stanislaus walked Gola around the La Salle College campus during the official recruiting trip. Brother Stanislaus was the president of La Salle College in 1952 (serving until 1958) and had taken over the position from Brother Gregorian Paul, who served as La Salle's president from 1945 to 1951. Brother Stanislaus appreciated athletics for a college and its campus. (He left the Christian Brothers in 1958, reverted to his legal name of Michael Duzy, and held administrative posts at several universities before retiring in 1993.)

"I had one conversation with Tom," Duzy said to *La Salle Magazine* in 1998. "We walked around the track. At the end of the conversation, I said, 'Tom, we'd very much like to have you at La Salle.' That's the only conversation I had with him."

Brother Stanislaus wanted to give La Salle an identity through sports, and specifically through the men's basketball team. He loved sports and wanted to increase the student body greatly following World War II. During his first few months as president, he realized that the students were not marketing La Salle and seemed not to be proud to attend the college.

"I realized that we had to give them [students] a good reason for being at La Salle and being happy about it," Duzy told *La Salle Magazine* in 1998. "I decided that basketball was key."

Gola also got a chance to spend time with some of the La Salle basketball players prior to making his final decision.

Gola told *La Salle Magazine* in 1994, "When I was in high school[,] I went over to New York to see La Salle in the NIT [National Invitation Tournament]. I stayed in the hotel room with Ace McCann and Larry Foust."

Robert "Ace" McCann played for the La Salle Explorers from 1946 to 1950 under head coaches Charles McGlone and Joe Meehan. McCann was a complete offensive and defensive player, who later served in the U.S. Navy. During his time at La Salle, his Explorer teams went 82–21 and made NIT appearances in 1948 and 1950. McCann was inducted into the La Salle Hall of Athletes in 1991. After his college career at 20th and Olney, Larry Foust was selected fifth overall by the Chicago Stags in the 1950 draft. The Chicago Stags franchise folded before the start of the 1950–1951 NBA season, and Foust joined the Fort Wayne Pistons. He later played for the Minneapolis Lakers and the St. Louis Hawks. In his twelve-year NBA career, Foust played in the All-Star game eight times.

La Salle's athletic director, Jim Henry, made a deal with the Gola family, offering any family members the same scholarship that Tom would receive to attend the college. Other schools pursuing Gola's skills did not consider giving his siblings financial help to attend school.

Guard Matt Fanning was a member of the 1951 La Salle College basketball team. He remembers the buzz surrounding Gola's recruitment. Fanning is also a Philadelphia native who grew up playing basketball at Kenney's in Wildwood, New Jersey.

"Everyone anticipated him coming, because of how good he was in high school," Fanning said.

The colors on Gola's jersey stayed the same: blue and gold. He picked La Salle College as his next destination.

3

....

La Salle College

*1952 NIT Championship
and 1953 Season*

DURING WORLD WAR II, the La Salle College student body
dropped to an all-time low of eighty-five students. The Christian
Brothers managed to keep the doors open, and in 1950, just five
years after the end of the war, more than twenty-three hundred young men
were pursuing a college education on the campus at 20th and Olney, thanks
in great measure to the GI Bill, which provided educational benefits to war
veterans.

In 1950, La Salle hired Ken Loeffler (pronounced "Leffler") as its new
head coach. Loeffler was from Beaver Falls, Pennsylvania, and had graduated from Penn State in 1924. After graduation, Loeffler became the head
basketball coach at Geneva College and later Yale, and he attended the
University of Pittsburgh Law School. During his time coaching and teaching at Yale, Loeffler was suitemates with then-student Gerald Ford, the future U.S. president. In 1942, Loeffler joined the U.S. Army Air Corps and
was discharged three years later. After serving in the office of the Assistant
Chief of the Air Staff at the Pentagon, Loeffler became the head coach of the
St. Louis Bombers in the Basketball Association of America (BAA).

Before he arrived at La Salle, Loeffler tallied seventeen years of coaching
experience at the college and professional levels. He took over at La Salle
when the previous head coach, Charles McGlone, resigned at the end of the

1948–1949 season to enter the private sector. Loeffler's three-man weave and flash-pivot style of play helped La Salle make it to the 1950 quarterfinals of the National Invitation Tournament (NIT) before losing to Duquesne. In Loeffler's second season, La Salle lost to St. Louis in the first round of the NIT. He was known as a disciplinarian who ran a strict program.

"He wanted every one of his players to be successful in life—not just in basketball," says Loeffler's son, Dusty.

During the 1951–1952 season, Gola's first at La Salle College, the La Salle Explorers rattled off eight straight wins to start the season before a 62–46 loss to seventh-ranked St. Louis, the same team that had defeated them the prior year in the NIT. The Explorers played again in the eight-day NIT in 1952, but they were up against powerhouse schools Dayton, Duquesne, Holy Cross, and St. Bonaventure. The NIT was the premier postseason tournament at the time—basically, the National Collegiate Athletic Association (NCAA) Tournament before the NCAA Tournament had any legs.

"The NIT was the big draw. [You were] lucky to get something written in the paper about being in the NCAA's [tournament]," says Ed Altieri, a member of the 1952 La Salle team.

The first NIT match-up for the Explorers was against the Seton Hall Pirates. Nobody really gave La Salle a chance in the first round. Seton Hall had Walter Dukes, who ranked in the top five in the country for rebounding. The Pirates had only two losses all year, so the Explorers were heavy underdogs.

"It made me angry to hear people say you will be back home after the first one," said La Salle captain Charles "Buddy" Donnelly in a self-published article in the *La Salle Collegian*. "So I decided that we weren't coming back after the Seton Hall game."

Donnelly and Gola took the Pirates by storm, taking down the heavy favorites 80–76. Gola, of course, led the way in his first postseason game, scoring a season-high 30 points.

"This was a new team, a young team, like a child, in fact," head coach Loeffler told the *La Salle Collegian* in March 1952. "It first had to walk. As a child would, it fell a few times. It gradually learned to walk, then to run. Against Seton Hall[,] it found it could jump as well as run. It had grown up."

Gola's second postseason game, which was the very next night, was one of the worst of his collegiate career. He did not score against St. John's until three minutes into the second half. Luckily, although Gola struggled,

Norm Grekin took control by hitting 13 of his 17 free throws, setting a tournament record. Grekin and the Explorers went to the line frequently, as both teams combined for 64 fouls, with 42 of those fouls committed by St. John's. The Redmen's top scorer, Robert "Zeke" Zawoluk, fouled out of the game, as did teammates Dick Duckett, Solly Walker, Jim Davis, and Ron MacGilvray. La Salle capitalized on the St. John's foul trouble and won the low-scoring game, 51–45, to advance to the semifinals. Gola finished the game with just 7 points.

Up next for La Salle in the semifinal game was the Duquesne Dukes and star players Jim Tucker and Dick Ricketts. La Salle won that game, 59–46, to advance to the championship final.

Madison Square Garden sold out all eighteen thousand seats for the championship game on March 16, 1952. For the second year in a row, the Dayton Flyers advanced to the NIT final, having lost in the 1951 final to Brigham Young University. Dayton was riding a hot streak, having not lost a game since December 29, 1951.

The Explorers raced out to a big lead, as much as 18 points, and ended up holding on for a 75–64 final score and their first NIT Championship. Gola led the way with 22 points, with Fred Iehle right behind him with 18. La Salle became the first school from Philadelphia to win the NIT since Temple won the inaugural tournament in 1938.

For the first time in NIT history, the Most Valuable Player (MVP) award was given to multiple players. Gola and Grekin shared the honor, and they joined Jack Moore, La Salle's only African American player that season, on the NIT First All-National Invitation Team. It was the first time three teammates were named to the team in the same year.

The celebration for the Explorers started immediately. Loeffler was reportedly on Ed Sullivan's *Toast of the Town* TV show on Sunday, March 16, the night La Salle won the NIT. The rest of the team got involved in the festivities when they returned the next day to a championship celebration with seventy-five cars riding through downtown Philadelphia. The parade route went from city hall to La Salle College and then back to city hall for a second time around. Accompanied by a police escort, the players got out of their vehicles to greet the four hundred students packing city hall. Students carried Donnelly on their shoulders with cheers of "Put Donnelly in Billy Penn's Place" and "Gola for Mayor," the latter a poignant foreshadowing of Gola's career. The cheers from the traffic-stopping caravan parade grew louder as the team progressed up and down Broad Street. Gola and Grekin were in a black convertible with the top down, sitting on top of the back seats with the "NIT Champs" sign hanging from the front of the bumper.

La Salle's athletic director, Jim Henry, took out a *Collegian* advertisement to give thanks to the members of the student body for their "wonderful support and splendid conduct" during the tournament.

On March 31, 1952, as a prize for winning the NIT, the La Salle Explorers were invited to try out for a chance to compete in the 1952 Summer Olympic Games in Helsinki, Finland. For the second time in less than a month, La Salle played St. John's, which had also been the runner-up in the NCAA Tournament; 1952 was the final year when teams could participate in the NIT and in the NCAA Tournament. La Salle beat St. John's 71–62 in the Olympic trials to advance to play Clyde Lovellette and the University of Kansas Jayhawks.

"We heard about them [La Salle] a lot," Lovellette said. "We didn't have any film on them, but we did have a scouting report."

Loeffler wanted his team on edge prior to the game against Kansas and was rumored to have enlisted Bill Mlkvy from Temple University, Ernie Beck from the University of Pennsylvania, and some Philadelphia Warriors to scrimmage with the Explorers.

Tensions were high prior to the game, with newspapers reporting that Kansas's head coach Dr. Forrest "Phog" Allen and Loeffler almost got in a fight at the teams' hotel when Loeffler, who is known to speak his mind, called the Jayhawks some variation of "hicks." This alleged incident caused some tense moments just hours before tip-off, although Lovellette does not remember the fight, nor does he recall seeing Allen ever lay a hand on anyone. He does recall that the Kansas teams were not fond of playing in New York City, the snake pit of college basketball during the early 1950s.

"We were country. We were proud to be from the Midwest," Lovellette says.

Allen was also worried about the referee situation for the game. He believed that Kansas would not have a shot at winning the game with two East Coast officials calling the game. Allen thought it would be only fair to have a geographically mixed group of referees monitor the game, and the Olympic committee agreed, replacing John Nucatola from Bayside, New York, with Ronald Gibbs from Springfield, Illinois.

The Explorers were at a disadvantage before the ball even tipped. Moore did not travel with La Salle to New York due to the death of his mother. Moore, who was an Overbrook High School alum, received support from within the La Salle community following this sudden loss.

"When my mother passed away, we were all in shock," he says. "It was totally unexpected. It was something unbelievable. She was in good health. As far as we knew, she didn't have any health problems."

Moore contemplated traveling with La Salle to New York, but he feared he would not be 100 percent ready for the game.

"I did want to play. But I don't think I was mentally able to do anything. I don't think my mind would have been in playing ball."

Loeffler had hoped to stick Moore on Lovellette to control rebounds. The Jayhawks ended up defeating La Salle, 70–65, at Madison Square Garden in front of eleven thousand people.

"We were so much better than them," La Salle's Altieri says.

Lovellette scored 40 points against the Explorers, the most points scored by a single player during the 1952 season.

"We were just playing strong basketball all the way through," Lovellette says.

With Kansas's win in the Olympic trial finals, seven of the fourteen members of the U.S. basketball team were from Lawrence, Kansas; the other seven players were from the Phillips 66ers, an amateur basketball team located in Bartlesville, Oklahoma. The American team played from July to August, winning eight straight games to capture the gold medal for the United States, with the Soviet Union winning silver and Uruguay winning bronze.

"My greatest thrill was to represent the United States in the Olympic Games. Of all of the championships I won in pros and in college, that was top of the list," Lovellette says.

La Salle's 1952 season was over, and the team lost two seniors to graduation. After Captain Donnelly and Newt Jones played their final games as Explorers, Loeffler had to make adjustments to his lineup for the next season.

The Explorers were early favorites to return to the NIT to repeat as champions in 1953. After a 20–5 record in the regular season, the Explorers secured a berth in the tournament. La Salle had a bye in the first round before again facing St. John's. St. John's beat St. Louis in the first round of the tourney to face the Explorers in the quarterfinals.

"We practically had the same team from the year before except for a couple of guys," says Altieri.

Injuries plagued Gola and Moore prior to the semifinal game. Moore was dealing with flu-related symptoms, and Gola had a bad ankle. Both players could play, but the real question was whether they could play to the best of their abilities with no hiccups. Moore and Gola suited up for the game but didn't start for the Explorers, instead entering the game in the second half.

"Tom came in the second half and was limping and hobbling around. His ankle was real bad," Altieri recalls.

Although Gola was not at 100 percent, he still tried to play at a competitive level for his teammates. Being on the court was better than not suiting up for the game at all. If anything, Gola's ability to play through his injury gave La Salle hope. La Salle was a totally different team without Gola, its tallest player, on the court, yet head coach Loeffler thought that it could survive without two of its best players.

"Loeffler thought that we could win without Tom," Altieri says.

Unfortunately, Loeffler's alternate game plan without Gola backfired. The Explorers found themselves down by 10 at the half, 43–33, and it struggled in an uphill battle for the rest of the game.

"We were behind, and [we were] playing catch-up," Moore says.

Playing from behind was something Gola and La Salle were not used to in 1953. St. John's led 74–71 with 1:20 left in the game. Moore drew a foul and went to the line, where he made the first attempt but missed the second. As the ball rimmed out, Gola leaped into the air and tipped the ball in, tying the game, 74–74, with 80 seconds left. With seconds remaining, La Salle's Altieri fouled St. John's Duckett, who made only one free throw. La Salle was down by 1 point.

La Salle had possession of the ball with 10 seconds left when Iehle was tackled underneath the basket, resulting in a foul. With pressure and time on his side, Iehle could win the game for the Explorers. Altieri walked up behind him to give a boost of confidence.

"You son of a bitch. Just think, Fred Iehle makes two foul shots to win the game," Altieri recalls telling Iehle at the foul line.

Altieri meant his words to Iehle as a joke, because he was confident that his teammate would make the two shots. But Iehle, who was noted as the best shooter on the team, missed not one but both shots. La Salle got the rebound and fed the ball to Gola, who was still in the game despite his injury. Gola couldn't get a shot off as time expired; the Explorers were eliminated from the 1953 NIT. Gola had scored 17 points in limited playing time. The St. John's upset was a big shock for everyone in attendance, even surprising the team's coach, Alfred (Dusty) DeStefano.

"I didn't think we had a chance of staying on the same court with La Salle. But the boys proved me wrong," DeStefano told the *Gettysburg Times* in 1953.

Newspapers reported that both coaches yelled at the officials, although they denied it after the game. St. John's went on to the championship game but lost to Seton Hall. The Explorers finished the season with a respectable 25–3 record, but with disappointment in light of their dreams to repeat as NIT champions.

"I didn't think they [St. John's] were much better, but it didn't matter because they won," laughs Dick Breen.

The 1953 season was Breen's last at La Salle. He had sat on the bench for the majority of his playing career at 20th and Olney, watching Gola from the sidelines. But even though he did not play much, being on the team with Gola was a profound experience.

"Two best years of my life was sitting on that bench and watching Tommy," Breen says. "It's hard to explain today just how great he was."

Even as a young sophomore, Gola found a way to make his legacy influence his fellow teammates at La Salle. In 1953, Gola played 28 games, averaging a team-best 18.5 points per game and 15.5 rebounds per game, resulting in his being named to the United Press International All-NIT first team, among several other honors.

4

....

1954 NCAA Champions

THE LA SALLE EXPLORERS were an inexperienced team in the fall of 1953. Nine of the twelve players on the team were sophomores, with only one senior player, guard Frank O'Hara. Tom Gola and O'Hara were named as the team captains. After a quick exit from the National Invitation Tournament (NIT) in the 1952–1953 season, the Explorers were eager to get back into postseason play.

La Salle kicked off its 1953–1954 season in an unusual spot: a high school gym. The Explorers played four games at the Abraham Lincoln High School gymnasium at Rowland and Ryan Avenues in Northeast Philadelphia during the 1954 season.

La Salle slated a 6–1 record before playing in the Kentucky Invitational in Lexington, Kentucky, in December 1953. La Salle played and defeated John Wooden's University of California, Los Angeles (UCLA) Bruins but lost to the University of Kentucky Wildcats, 73–60. The 1954 Kentucky Wildcats went undefeated that season, with a record of 24–0, and 14–0 in the Southeastern Conference. Kentucky was not eligible for postseason play that year because three players, Cliff Hagan, Frank Ramsey, and Lou Tsioropoulos, were attending graduate school. At that time, National Collegiate Athletic Association (NCAA) rules prohibited graduate students from participating in postseason competition.

After losing to Kentucky, the Explorers played in the Holiday Festival Tournament at Madison Square Garden, with wins against St. Louis and Brigham Young and one loss to Niagara. The La Salle team started to gel at the end of December, as the Explorers rode an eleven-game winning streak into the second week of February. Gola put up monster numbers in 1954, with team highs in scoring, including 41 points against Loyola and 31 rebounds against Brigham Young. Before getting a berth in the NCAA Tournament, La Salle had a 21–4 record.

The first team standing in the Explorers' way in the 1954 NCAA Tournament was Fordham. The Rams were an experienced team, having won eighteen or more games in each of the previous four seasons, which included an NCAA Tournament berth in 1953. La Salle had to travel to Buffalo, New York, for the game, which was played at Memorial Auditorium.

The game was close from start to finish. Fordham scored with just over four seconds left in the game to jump out to a 2-point lead. Coach Loeffler was notorious throughout his coaching career for calling time-outs toward the end of the game. Against Fordham, Loeffler called not one but two time-outs that ended up saving the Explorers' season. La Salle's Charlie Greenberg called a time-out at mid-court just after Fordham's basket put the Rams ahead. After the time-out, La Salle scrambled to run a play, but Greenberg again called time-out.

"I thought of something and had to run back to the coach and get another time-out," Greenberg says.

The Explorers were moments away from going home.

"Had we not . . . called that time-out, it would have been a hustle shot," Frank Blatcher says. "It was a brilliant move by Loeffler."

During the time-out, Loeffler drew up a play for Gola to come off a long pivot and have Greenberg screen Gola's defender to give him room to shoot.

"The pass was supposed to go to Gola, who was supposed to shoot it," Greenberg says.

The plan didn't work from the start. Instead, O'Hara passed the ball to Gola, but the pass was almost deflected by a Rams player. Gola grabbed the ball and spotted teammate Fran O'Malley cutting from the right side of the court for an easy lay-up. The Explorers tied the game, 68–68, the eleventh tie of the game. The game went into overtime.

A thirty-five-foot jumper by Charlie Singley and two free throws from

Gola put the Explorers in the lead early in the overtime period. La Salle held the lead for the rest of the game, even though Fordham had a chance to tie at the end. A last-second shot by Fordham's Ed Conlin missed, and La Salle survived with a 76–74 win. Gola scored 28 points.

"That game I'll never forget. They had the talent to beat us, and we were down with four seconds to go. But our guys had gained some confidence and poise by then. After we pulled it out, we were ready for anybody," Gola told *La Salle Magazine* in 1974.

After the game, La Salle's Blatcher quickly left Buffalo because he got word that his father was not doing well back home. He and his sister, who had attended the game, took a train back to 30th Street Station in Philadelphia. Blatcher called home from the train station to learn that his father, Frank Blatcher Sr., had passed away from a strangulated hernia that exploded intestinally.

"It was a traumatic time for me. It was very tough," Blatcher says.

A few days later, La Salle was slated to play North Carolina State at the Palestra. The funeral for Blatcher's father was Friday morning, just hours before the Explorers' next tournament game versus the Wolfpack. The services took place at the Blatchers' home in South Philadelphia near Washington Avenue, where every player, coach, and even La Salle's athletic director, Jim Henry, was in attendance. Once the players and staff had paid their respects to the family, the team proceeded to the Palestra. Being the youngest of thirteen kids (eight girls and five boys), Blatcher debated not playing in the game against the Wolfpack, but he eventually left to join his team.

"I was trying to make a decision whether to play or not. I'm from a big family, and the team was expecting me to play," Blatcher says.

La Salle needed Blatcher's outside shooting presence against North Carolina State, which was on a ten-game winning streak, including the Atlantic Coast Conference (ACC) Tournament. La Salle had faced the Wolfpack earlier in the 1954 regular season, winning 83–78. In this game, Gola had broken a La Salle scoring record, with 1,449 points in a season. Now Gola guarded North Carolina State sophomore Ronnie Shavlik, who was the same height as Gola.

La Salle got off to a rough start in the first period. They were 5-for-19 from the field, but the teams still managed to trade the lead seven times in the first half. The Explorers led by 1 point at the half, 36–35.

The game was close until the final two minutes, when La Salle poured in 17 points to run away with an 88–81 win. Gola and Singley combined for 52 points.

For the second straight NCAA Tournament game, the Explorers would play at the Palestra, this time against the Naval Academy. The game was also the second tournament game at the Palestra for the Midshipmen, having defeated Cornell, 69–67, in the prior round. The game in Philadelphia was a homecoming for Navy's senior Ned Hogan, who had attended West Catholic High School.

Senior Bill Hoover started for Navy in the 1954 game against La Salle. The Chicago native knew that height was going to be the biggest headache for the Midshipmen.

"There maybe was a height restriction in the Navy, at that time, of . . . 6 ft. 4. Our center was [nevertheless] maybe 6 ft. 6. [Even so,] for us to play against a team that had a 6 ft. 6 guard in Tom Gola was kind of a mismatch to start with," Hoover says.

College basketball had never seen a player of Gola's 6 ft. 6 in. height with the ability to rebound *and* to dribble a basketball effectively. His height was an obstacle for opponents, but his quickness and agility created a recipe for disaster. Seven of the twelve players for Navy were walk-ons in 1954. Because the Navy team was not the tallest in the country, its game plan was to push the ball in transition and outrun any opponents. The pace affected the Explorers, who opened the game shooting 17.5 percent from the field in the first half, which resulted in a 21-all tie. Gola had 13 of those 21 points at the half.

"We knew it was going to be a tough game," Hoover says. "I think we were probably happy to be in it at halftime, and I think we felt that we could probably have stayed in it. But the height advantage was an issue. Gola was tough to stop for us."

The "Olneynites," as the *Collegian* called the Explorers that year, caught fire in the third period, stretching out to a 44–29 lead. (College basketball games were played in four ten-minute quarters between 1951 and 1954.) The Navy offense was led by Don Lange and John Clune, whom La Salle shut down in the second half.

"La Salle double-teamed both Clune and Lange and basically let the rest of the three guards run around. La Salle knew the guards weren't going to shoot and that we weren't accustomed to shooting. That's how they defended us," Hoover explains.

The Explorers kept the foot on the gas after the double team seemed to work and ended up winning the game by 20 points, 68–48. Gola finished the game with 22 points and 24 rebounds. This rebounding for the Explorers made all the difference.

"That's a huge number!" Hoover says. "I'm a 6 ft. 2 guard. [Larry] Wigley and I only had eight rebounds apiece. That was the most on the team."

The Explorers out-rebounded Navy 56 to 36, which Hoover believes was the biggest factor in Navy's losing the game. Gola's tough defense against Lange worked, as Lange could score only 3 points.

"I ended up [in] my high school days losing to Gola in the Palestra and [in] my college days losing to him again in the Palestra," Hogan says.

For the first time in the school's history, La Salle made it to the Final Four.

The Final Four of the 1954 NCAA Tournament included La Salle, Penn State, Bradley, and the University of Southern California. The Explorers held a light workout on campus prior to driving to Philadelphia International Airport to head to Kansas City, Missouri, to play at the Municipal Auditorium. "The Moxie Kids from 20th and Olney," as the *Collegian* called them in the school newspaper, were greeted at the airport by hundreds of fans. They set up a walking tunnel for the players as they boarded the plane, and the team was presented with double shamrocks from the city of Philadelphia as good luck tokens for the big game.

La Salle's next opponent was Ken Loeffler's alma mater, Penn State. Loeffler had been a student at Happy Valley from 1920 to 1924. He believed that Penn State's success thus far in the tournament was largely due to its zone defense. The only problem with playing zone for the Nittany Lions was the question of how to guard Gola.

"We knew through the scouting report that this guy [Gola] was the real McCoy. He was the best [I'd] seen all season long," says Rudy Marisa, a sophomore on the 1954 Penn State team.

In a low-scoring first half, La Salle held a 33–22 lead heading into the locker rooms. The Explorers had the lead, but the full court press from Penn State was getting to them.

"Everyone knew what we were going to do, but if we did it well[,] nobody [could] beat us," Marisa says.

To beat the press, Loeffler had Gola working the fast pivot. He would receive the inbound pass and then quickly throw the ball down the court over the press. Penn State's zone was a three-man front, full-zone press that transitioned to a sliding zone.

"That's the first time I've seen a full court press as good as that," Blatcher recalls.

Penn State tried to press La Salle, but it didn't work. Penn State kept switching from a press to a regular 3-on-2 defense, then to a man-to-man. With the defense packed in tight, La Salle shooters Blatcher and Singley had the opportunity to shoot from the outside. La Salle won the game, 69–54. Gola and Blatcher led the way with 19 points apiece, and Gola also had 19 rebounds.

The Explorers were moving on to the NCAA championship game against Bradley. Philadelphia's mayor, Joseph Clark, and Philadelphia council member Jim Finnegan sent a wire to the La Salle team in Kansas City, wishing them good luck moving forward.

For Bradley to have reached the NCAA Tournament was a huge accomplishment for the program, as three years earlier the Braves had been involved in the 1951 gambling scandal that sent shockwaves through the NCAA. Five Bradley players—Gene Melchiorre, Bill Mann, Charles "Bud" Grover, Aaron Preece, and Jim Kelly—had admitted to taking bribes from gamblers to control the score against St. Joseph's and Oregon State during the 1951 season. A total of seven schools and thirty-two players had been tainted by the scandal, with some facing jail. Bradley's Melchiorre, Mann, and George Chinankos had received suspended sentences, while Grover, Preece, Kelly, and Fred Schlictman had been acquitted. The sanctions against the basketball team had resulted in a two-year ban from postseason play. The 1954 season was only expected to serve as a fresh start for the program, but it ended with a trip to the NCAA championship game. The 15–12 Bradley team was basketball's Cinderella in 1954.

The 1954 NCAA Tournament included a number of firsts. It was the first time the championship team had to overcome five opponents to win the title. It was also the first nationally televised game in the history of the NCAA. NBC reportedly paid $7,500 for the national broadcast TV rights.

Bradley senior Ed King guarded Gola in the championship game. Heading into the big game, King and his teammates knew that Gola was a special player and what to expect from him. Prior to the game, Bradley's coach, Forrest "Forddy" Anderson, told his team to focus on the game and nothing else: literally. During pregame introductions, Coach Anderson told his players not to even look at La Salle while the starting lineups were announced.

"Coach wanted us to stay within ourselves and the huddle. [But] the whole team was doing what they shouldn't have been doing, watching La Salle," King recalls.

Not many La Salle fans were in attendance due to the distance from Philadelphia to Kansas City. The Braves dominated the first twenty minutes and led by as many as 7 points early in the second period, yet La Salle fought back to just a 2-point deficit, 44–42, at halftime. Gola was in foul trouble early with 4 fouls, which caused Loeffler to have to make some adjustments on defense while Gola sat on the bench.

"We were feeling pretty good about ourselves, being 2 points up, but in the second half, Gola took over," King says.

Gola made sure there would be no drama in La Salle's first national championship in school history. La Salle outscored Bradley 30–14 in the third quarter, which paved the way to the 92–76 win for La Salle. For the first time in the school's history, La Salle College was the national champion.

Blatcher and Singley led all scorers with 23 points apiece, while Gola had 19. As King was leaving the court, having fouled out, Gola went up to him to shake his hand.

"He was a real sportsman on the floor. He was a man who automatically commanded attention, and it was a pleasure to be able to be on the floor with him [and] to watch him take over that game," King says.

The champion Explorers were treated with pomp and circumstance on their way back to Philadelphia from Kansas City. An estimated ten thousand fans were on hand when the Explorers touched down at Philadelphia International Airport. La Salle student John Nark had listened to the championship game on the radio back in Philadelphia. He remembers how excited the city was when La Salle returned from Kansas City with the national championship.

"They were the toast of the town when they came back," Nark says.

La Salle fans flooded the airport and escorted the team back to Olney for a rally at the campus field house. The field house rally featured pep talks from O'Hara and Gola, speaking on behalf of the team. James Finnegan, the president of the city council; Brother Erminus Stanislaus, La Salle's president; and Father Mark Heath, the college chaplain, all attended, with

William Wingle, the president of the student council, serving as the master of ceremonies. To top off the championship victory, cake and coffee were handed out to fans in attendance.

On March 22, 1954, Mayor Clark officially proclaimed "La Salle Day" in Philadelphia in recognition of the Explorers' accomplishments. As part of "La Salle Day," co-captains O'Hara and Gola accepted a gold seal of the city on behalf of their teammates.

Following La Salle's victory over Bradley, the NCAA named Gola the Outstanding Collegiate Basketball Player, and the Philadelphia Sports Writers Association honored Loeffler as Coach of the Year at its awards dinner.

The final Associated Press basketball poll listed La Salle as the second-ranked team in the nation, a scant 32 points behind Kentucky. The Wildcats that year went undefeated, but three of their best players were fifth-year players and therefore ineligible to compete in the NCAA Tournament. Kentucky's coach, Adolph Rupp, decided not to have his team participate in tournament play. La Salle earned 33 first-place votes among the sports writers.

Gola added another accolade when the Helms Athletic Foundation chose him as the Basketball Player of the Year in 1954. As the player of the year, Gola received the Paul H. Helms trophy, and his name was engraved on the Hall of Fame trophy in Helms Hall in Los Angeles. La Salle student Thomas Dougherty, class of 1955, recalls Gola's tenure at 20th and Olney.

"He floated across the court. He was so smooth. He was poetry in motion. I liken him to guys in other sports, like Joe DiMaggio. He always looked like he was playing effortlessly," Dougherty says.

Gola was the first La Salle player to win the Helms Award since its inception in 1920. Other notable winners include Kansas's Clyde Lovellette, Villanova's Paul Arizin, Yale's Tony Lavelli, and St. Joseph's College's George Senesky.

By leading La Salle to an NIT title and an NCAA Championship in his first three collegiate seasons, Gola had set the bar very high. The ultimate challenge that awaited the Explorers in his senior season would rise just as tall.

5

....

1955

Gola versus K.C. Jones and Bill Russell

IN MAY 1954, the University of Pennsylvania proposed that the four surrounding universities and colleges in the Philadelphia area—La Salle College, Temple University, Villanova University, and St. Joseph's College—play their basketball games on the campus of the University of Pennsylvania at the Palestra. This commitment would help Penn bear the costs of maintaining the arena, which would become a hallowed hall in the history of college basketball and lay the foundation for years of intracity rivalries. In 1955, the Palestra expanded to 9,100 seats. On November 23, 1954, the University of Pennsylvania's president, Dr. Gaylord Harnwell, announced the formation of the Big 5, an official league for the five Philadelphia schools. The 1955–1956 season marked the start of the Big 5 on December 14, as Villanova faced off against St. Joseph's at the Palestra.

After Tom Gola's heroic championship-leading run in 1954, he was named the team captain heading into the 1954–1955 season. La Salle lost only one player following its championship season, when Frank O'Hara was drafted by the Philadelphia Warriors in round 11 of the 1954 NBA draft.

"We were a better team in 1955 than in 1954. Two reasons: Gola was better, and all of [the] sophomores were now juniors. We lost one guy who was 5 ft. 6 in O'Hara and picked up Alonzo Lewis, who was bigger," Frank Blatcher says.

Lewis came from Upper Darby High School in Drexel Hill, Pennsylvania, where he scored 1,048 points. He was the second African American basketball player to play for La Salle, following Jack Moore during the 1952 and 1953 seasons. Lewis was a complete player, who added versatility with his ball-handling skills and his ability to rebound and defend. La Salle also added four more players in 1955: Joe Gilson, Walt Fredericks, Bob Kraemer, and John Gola, Tom's younger brother.

For the third consecutive year, La Salle kicked off its season against Millersville. In their first five games of the season, the Explorers went undefeated before losing to fifteenth-ranked Utah, 79–69, at Madison Square Garden. For the second year in a row, Gola and the Explorers participated in the Kentucky Invitational in Lexington, Kentucky. La Salle defeated Southern California but lost to the number-one team in the country at the time, the Kentucky Wildcats.

"I honestly think if we [had] played them [Kentucky] at the end of the year, we would have beaten them," Blatcher recalls.

La Salle also played in the Holiday Festival Tournament at Madison Square Garden against Syracuse; the University of California, Los Angeles (UCLA); and Duquesne. Gola was named the most valuable player of the tournament. During his four years at La Salle, Gola won fifteen of nineteen games played at Madison Square Garden, where he averaged 20 points and 18 rebounds per game. His greatest game at the Garden came against Syracuse in 1954, where he scored 34 points and grabbed 26 rebounds. Gola achieved a team-best 37 rebounds against Lebanon Valley College in January, a game that also included La Salle's largest point total in 1955, 112–70. La Salle rode a nine-game winning streak before its postseason trip into the NCAA Tournament, managing a 22–4 record before postseason play.

The Explorers kicked off the NCAA Tournament against the West Virginia Mountaineers at Madison Square Garden. La Salle was looking to become the first team to repeat as national champions since the 1948 and 1949 Adolph Rupp–led Kentucky Wildcats. The opening game between the Explorers and the Mountaineers was the first time the schools played against each other and the first NCAA Tournament appearance for West Virginia.

Despite great shooting by West Virginia guard Rod "Hot Rod" Hundley, La Salle held a 40–33 lead at the half. The Explorers came out in the second half in a zone defense, which rapidly increased their lead; La Salle walked away with a 95–61 victory. Hundley finished the game with 17 points, while La Salle's Lewis and Gola each had 22 points. Gola added 16 rebounds as well.

La Salle next faced the Princeton Tigers in the semifinal game at the Palestra. In their first eight games of the year in 1955, the Tigers went 1–7, but they turned their season around and won the final Eastern Intercollegiate Basketball League (EIBL) championship game to qualify for the NCAA Tournament. The following year, the EIBL would become the Ivy League.

Princeton's captain, Harold "Bud" Haabestad, knew that La Salle was going to be a tough opponent in the semifinals.

"Everyone anticipated [that] La Salle was going the distance," Haabestad says.

Haabestad, a Drexel Hill, Pennsylvania, native, remembers telling his coach, Franklin Cappon, to put a smaller guard on Gola to help eliminate his quickness on the court.

"Tom did not have a difficult time scoring, because he was always playing against someone who was bigger [than] or as big [as] and even slower [than he was]. Not that anyone could guard [Gola], but my theory was to put a smaller man on him," Haabestad says.

Instead, the Tigers took a different strategic direction. Princeton matched Gola's height with Richard Batt, while Haabestad guarded La Salle's Charlie Greenberg. La Salle beat Princeton 73–46, thanks in part to Gola's 24 points. Haabestad finished with 15 points in the loss, his last game in a Princeton uniform.

"He [Gola] was probably the best player I stepped on the court with," he says. "It was a thrill for me to come out to a packed place like the Palestra and to be shaking hands with Tom Gola and being in the NCAA Tournament. It was as good as it gets."

Next up for the Explorers was Canisius College from Buffalo, New York, again at the Palestra. The Explorers dominated the Golden Griffins from the start on their way to an easy 99–64 win, the largest margin of victory of Gola's NCAA Tournament career. After Tom's brother John came off the bench for La Salle and scored the 99th point, Canisius did its best to keep La Salle from breaking 100 points: the Golden Griffins began to hold the ball with four minutes left in the game. The Palestra crowd booed and covered the floor with programs and trash, interfering with the players and causing the referees to stop the game.

The 99–64 win against Canisius was La Salle's twelfth straight victory and its twenty-fifth of the season overall. In his final college appearance in a La Salle uniform in Philadelphia, Gola scored 30 points, grabbed 25 rebounds, and blocked a half dozen shots. La Salle's Lewis and Charlie Singley chipped in with 16 points each, and Greenberg scored 14. La Salle's victory lifted the Explorers to a second consecutive Final Four appearance.

That year, Gola was not the only La Salle student making a name for himself through sports. His classmate, Al Cantello, was gaining recognition in track and field, primarily for the javelin throw. Cantello, a native of Norristown, Pennsylvania, formed a good relationship with Gola while taking the same economics class. Throughout their time together at 20th and Olney, Gola and Cantello would be seen playing the harmonica and the guitar in the basement of College Hall on La Salle's campus.

"Tom was an icon. He was indigenous to Philadelphia and was the face of La Salle athletics," Cantello says. "Tom on the surface was unflappable. That was a tremendous asset to the press. They considered him humble and a resident competitor. I was way down the food chain. We shared four years with each other and got very close."

After his 1955 graduation from La Salle, Cantello broke the world record in the javelin throw at the 1959 Compton Invitational in Southern California. Cantello went on to become an Olympian, and he also won a bronze medal in the 1959 Pan American Games in Chicago, Illinois.

Hank DeVincent was another La Salle athlete making a name for himself in the 1950s. Prior to enrolling at La Salle, DeVincent played baseball at Olney High School. DeVincent's decision to attend La Salle, like Gola's, was highly influenced by the Christian Brothers.

"La Salle not only gave me an opportunity to go to college," said DeVincent in *La Salle Magazine* in 1989, "but after losing my father, the Brothers acted as a good parental influence. I have an extra affection for La Salle."

His career at La Salle had a false start, as DeVincent came down with hepatitis shortly after enrolling; he had to drop out of school until he recovered. DeVincent became an All-American outfielder for the La Salle baseball team, hitting .400 during his career. As a senior in 1956, DeVincent was captain of the baseball and the soccer teams, while also participating on the track and field team. After his graduation, DeVincent was drafted by the Cincinnati Reds, but he later retired from professional baseball to attend medical school. DeVincent was inducted into the La Salle Hall of Athletes in 1967. On April 29, 1978, La Salle named its baseball field the "Hank DeVincent Field." Today, the field is home to the La Salle Explorers baseball team, the La Salle Club baseball team, and the La Salle field hockey program.

Ira Davis was a member of the La Salle track and field team in the 1950s. Davis had played basketball and run track at Overbrook High School. At La Salle, Davis excelled as a triple jumper, an event in which he represented the United States in the Olympic Games in 1956 (Melbourne), 1960 (Rome), and 1964 (Tokyo). He broke several La Salle track and field records and once held the American record for the triple jump with 53 ft. 11 in. In 1964, he was selected for *Sport Magazine*'s All-Time Track and Field Team.

All that athletic greatness on La Salle's campus attracted some attention across the world of sports. Days prior to the 1955 Final Four game, several Major League Baseball (MLB) teams reached out to Gola, all bidding for his services after graduation. The Philadelphia Phillies, the Cincinnati Reds, the newly relocated Kansas City Athletics, and the New York Yankees were all interested in Gola's possible career in baseball.

"Sounds good," Gola told the *Philadelphia Inquirer*. "I've played some softball lately and a little baseball with Incarnation Catholic Club but I'd need a lot of practice. I played the outfield and first base."

Gola was not sure why these recruiters were calling, because he had never said he wanted to switch from basketball to baseball. The rumors started with John "Jocko" Collins, a supervisor of referees for the National Basketball Association (NBA) and a scout for the Philadelphia Phillies. A top Phillies official told Collins to find out whether Gola would be interested in working with the National League franchise. Word got out, and other teams joined in the chatter. Gola hadn't played baseball since his sophomore year of high school, yet baseball executives were saying that Gola had the makings of a star. Ultimately, nothing ever came of this speculation about Gola's playing MLB.

After these rumors started to subside, Gola still had a Final Four to play in. The 1955 Final Four in Kansas City, Missouri, included La Salle, Iowa, the University of San Francisco, and Colorado. It was the first National

Collegiate Athletic Association (NCAA) tournament appearance for Iowa and San Francisco.

The semifinals pitted the Explorers against Iowa. The game was close throughout, and Iowa's hot shooting forced Coach Ken Loeffler to switch to a 1-3-1 zone to start the second half. La Salle ended up winning the close, sloppy game, 76–73.

"We've probably never played as badly as we did at times tonight," Loeffler told the *Philadelphia Inquirer* after the game. "We had them down several times and we let them come back on us. When it got tough, the rest of the boys were depending too much on Gola."

Gola finished the game against Iowa with 23 points, and Singley scored 16.

"We just couldn't stop him [Gola]," says Bill Seaberg, a player on the 1955 Iowa Hawkeyes team. "He dominated the game offensively. He kind of demoralized us because he didn't miss a whole lot."

Gola scored 16 points in the first half and played with 4 personal fouls in the final five minutes of the game.

"In the second half, he [Gola] turned it on with his offensive ability. He just knew when to take over a game, and he did it for his team. We couldn't keep up with him," Seaberg adds.

La Salle dominated offensively throughout the tournament, outscoring its first four opponents 343–244. For the second-straight year, La Salle played in the NCAA Tournament championship game. The Explorers prepared to get a taste of West Coast basketball with Bill Russell, K.C. Jones, and the San Francisco Dons, who had defeated Colorado, 62–50.

"We didn't know who the hell San Francisco was," La Salle's Blatcher says. "I didn't know who K.C. Jones was or who Bill Russell was until we played them."

Just a few days before the national championship game, the Daub Jewelry Store on 5706 North 5th Street in Philadelphia filled its window with Gola's awards, plaques, medals, basketballs, and photos to celebrate his success.

"You never knew he was a celebrity. He was just another guy in class that had to go to basketball practice, and that was it," La Salle's classmate John Nark says, reinforcing Gola's odd mix of fame and obscurity.

The Dons arrived at the national championship game as the favorite to win the title. The Explorers felt confident, having won nine straight tournament games dating back to 1954 tourney, while San Francisco was working on its twenty-sixth straight win of the 1955 season.

A day prior to the championship game in Kansas City, the La Salle team went to see a movie after their final practice.

"I was the first one up at the box office and they wouldn't let me in," Lewis says in the book *Palestra Pandemonium: A History of the Big 5,* by Robert Lyons. "I hailed a cab and told the driver, 'Take me to the black pool room.' I got to the pool room and inside were Bill Russell, K.C. Jones and the other San Francisco players as well as two black players from Iowa. We played a couple of eight-ball games. I was probably a better shooter than all of them."

Lewis was not permitted to stay at the same hotel as his La Salle teammates. Earlier in the season, while playing Loyola in New Orleans, Lewis had become the first African American player to compete against white players in an athletic event in the state of Louisiana. The Explorers won that game, 85–71.

San Francisco was ranked number one in the country at the time, and La Salle was ranked second.

"I'm not worrying about Gola, I'm just trying to help my team win," Russell said to *Sports Illustrated* in 1955. "But, man, that Gola would really give the coach an ulcer."

La Salle would have to worry about Russell, who was a 6 ft. 10 in. center and the best two-way player in college basketball in 1955. The Explorers' usual script was flipped in the championship game, as Gola was only the second-best player on the court in the final.

"I think we just can't let the big guy get the ball. Once he gets his hands on it, he shoots. We can stop him only by keeping the ball away from him," Loeffler told *Sports Illustrated* in 1955.

San Francisco's head coach, Phil Woolpert, thought about having Russell guard Gola, but after speaking with his coaching staff, he decided to have point guard Jones take him on. Jones was 6 ft. 1 in. and 202 pounds, while Gola was six inches taller. But with Gola being guarded by someone matching his speed on the court, Russell could dominate underneath the basket. La Salle's Fran O'Malley guarded Russell.

"The strategy of putting K.C. on Gola was a stroke of genius. That way, Russell could stay around the basket and rebound," San Francisco senior Stan Buchanan recalls of the 1955 Dons.

"The game was billed as 'Gola the Great' against 'Russell the Remarkable,' but the outcome turned on the inspired play of another player, USF's [the University of San Francisco's] K.C. Jones," says Bernie Schneider, the historian of the San Francisco Dons basketball team.

From the first tip, in which Russell outstretched Gola, San Francisco controlled the game. La Salle played Gola on a roving basis and tried a sliding zone defense without much success, as Jones held Gola to just 9 points in the first half. The Dons were winning at the half, 36–24, thanks to the tag team of Russell and Jones.

"We felt like we were in control right from the start of the game. For some reason, and I don't know what it was, but it seemed like we beat them easy. It was just one of those things," says Rudy Zannini, a member of the 1955 San Francisco team.

The Explorers tried mounting a comeback in the second half, but San Francisco had an answer for each Explorer run. The Dons worked the high post the entire game, and Russell went unstopped in the paint. La Salle switched from 3–2 to 2–3 zones to try to limit Russell, but nothing was effective.

"They could inbound over the basket to Russell for a dunk," Schneider says.

San Francisco won the championship game, 77–63. For the first time in thirteen years, a Pacific Coast team took home the national title. Jones led all scorers with 24 points on 10-for-23 shooting from the field. Russell added 23 points and 25 rebounds. For the first time in the history of the NCAA, three African American players won a national championship and started for the winning team: Harold "Hal" Perry, K.C. Jones, and Bill Russell.

"They'd probably beat us nine out of 10 times simply because of Russell's height and leaping ability," Loeffler told the *Philadelphia Inquirer* after the 1955 loss. "You'd have to play perfect ball to beat them."

Gola finished the game with 16 points and 18 rebounds, his lowest scoring total of his NCAA Tournament career, while Singley led La Salle in scoring with 20.

"K.C. was the difference-maker, I think. He was a strong guy. Without him, they wouldn't have been as good," La Salle's Greenberg says.

Russell set a five-game NCAA scoring record of 118 points in the 1955 tournament, a record set by Gola just a year earlier when he scored a total of 114 points in 1954. The NCAA All-Tournament Committee named Russell the tourney's Most Valuable Player (MVP), making him the first African American player to be honored with the award. Russell and Gola were also added to the All-Tournament Team with K.C. Jones, Carl Cain of the University of Iowa, and Jim Ranglos of the University of Colorado.

"He [Gola] was a stately, good-looking, under-control guy. I had nothing but respect for him. I had the feeling he was a real gentleman. That was my feeling about him," recalls San Francisco's Buchanan.

At age thirty-nine, Woolpert became the youngest coach in the NCAA to win a championship. (Indiana University's head coach Bob Knight would break that record in 1976, when his Hoosiers defeated Michigan in Philadelphia at the Spectrum to win the NCAA Tournament.) The game of basketball changed in 1955 thanks to Russell and the San Francisco Dons, who won back-to-back national titles in 1955 and 1956. In 1956, the San Francisco Dons went 29–0, defeating Iowa in the final championship game. In his final season with the Dons, Russell was named the Helms Foundation College Basketball Player of the Year. Russell was later selected second overall by the St. Louis Hawks in the 1956 NBA Draft in New York. The Hawks would later trade Russell's draft rights to the Boston Celtics in exchange for Ed Macauley and Cliff Hagan.

The La Salle Explorers headed back to Philadelphia, with thousands of supporters welcoming their arrival at Philadelphia International Airport. The team, carrying the runner-up cup, walked off the plane to loving cheers. Police escorted the Explorers back to campus, where they attended a small reception with the student body.

After the 1955 season, Loeffler left 20th and Olney to coach at Texas A&M, a decision that came as a surprise to the La Salle Athletic Department. He posted 114 wins and 25 losses during his time with La Salle, with the 1952 season being his best, with 27 wins. La Salle reportedly offered Loeffler a new contract after the 1955 season, but he turned it down. In his six years at La Salle, Loeffler won the city title six times, with a winning percentage of .815.

Gola and his girlfriend, Caroline, got married at the Blessed Sacrament Church in Washington, D.C., on June 25, 1955. Twenty-four hours after Gola's wedding, he and Loeffler embarked on a trip sponsored by the State Department, traveling to eleven different countries in South America. Caroline also accompanied them, but Gola paid for her travel expenses himself.

"The very next day. You talk about a honeymoon!" Caroline laughs.

The tour started on June 27, with appearances in Mexico, Guatemala, Nicaragua, Panama, Peru, Chile, Argentina, Uruguay, Brazil, Haiti, and Puerto Rico, ending in the second week of August.

"Mexico City was the first time I ever met Loeffler," Caroline says.

The trip was a campaign to combat Communism and promote democracy within the Latin American countries by teaching various basketball clinics. The basketball clinics were primarily held in the afternoon, so the newlyweds got nights to themselves to sightsee and explore. Loeffler had to be back in the United States at the end of August to attend another clinic at the University of Connecticut. He would then head to Germany for a month-long tour with the Armed Forces, again teaching basketball.

Bob Ames, one of Gola's teammates in 1954 and 1955, would later become a popular figure in the U.S. military. Ames enlisted in the U.S. Army after his graduation in 1956 and later joined the Central Intelligence Agency (CIA), specializing in Middle East operations. Ames would later play a key role in developing the Ronald Reagan administration's peace initiative overseas and serve as the director of the CIA's Office of Analysis for the Near East and South Asia. Ames was killed on April 18, 1983, when the U.S. Embassy in Beirut, Lebanon, was bombed.

And just like that, Gola's time with Loeffler and La Salle was over. The 1955 season was statistically Gola's best of his collegiate career. He played in 31 games and scored 750 points, averaging 24.2 points per game. He still holds La Salle records in free throws attempted (267) and free throws made (202) during the 1955 season. In his four years and 118 games played at La Salle College, Gola scored 2,462 points and pulled down an NCAA record 2,201 rebounds, a record that has stood for more than a half century. From December 2, 1953, to January 29, 1955, Gola recorded 48 straight double-doubles, an NCAA record. Gola won 102 of 121 games he played at La Salle. But now, the Tom Gola era was over.

La Salle's coaching search for Loeffler's replacement was quick, with thirty-three-year-old Jim Pollard, just retired from playing for the NBA's Minneapolis Lakers, taking over for the Explorers. Pollard had played eight years with the Minneapolis Lakers and won four NBA titles during his tenure, with the help of teammates George Mikan and Vern Mikkelsen. Prior to accepting the coaching position at La Salle, Pollard turned down several lucrative radio and television offers in his hometown of Minneapolis, the *Collegian* reported in April 1955. Pollard accepted a three-year contract on April 13, 1955, and in that time posted a 48–28 record but never reached postseason play with the Explorers. Donald "Dudey" Moore replaced Pollard as head coach at La Salle in 1959.

6

. . . .

Love Letters and
Wildwood

I N THE SUMMER OF 1951, in North Wildwood, Tom Gola fell in love
with Caroline Norris of Washington, D.C.

"We would sit on the beach all day. That's the way it was," Caroline
recalls.

Tom was heading into his first year at La Salle College, and Caroline
was entering her senior year at Theodore Roosevelt High School in the
nation's capital. Caroline's grandfather, Joseph Kieffer, owned a beach
home on 23rd and Surf in North Wildwood.

"I went down to Wildwood, and I did nothing," Caroline says. "All I
did was go on the beach at ten o'clock in the morning, catch up with [my
friend] Eileen, come home at five o'clock, eat my dinner, take a shower, and
go on the boardwalk."

Caroline first met "Tommy" through her friend Eileen Ryan (now Eileen
Farrell).

"He thought she was the greatest thing since Coca-Cola," Farrell says.

After a summer of hanging out, Caroline's watching Tom play ball,
and hitting the boardwalk together every night, their relationship blossomed. After a year of getting to know each other, Tom would write to
Caroline, who was then entering her first year at Marymount College.
Tom was a crafty writer, to say the least, writing two- to three-page letters

talking about anything and everything and even making up his own fairy tales.

"He wrote beautifully," Caroline says. "He had a talent to write."

Caroline did not have the slightest clue that she was in a long-distance relationship with a popular college basketball player. To her credit, she didn't care about his popularity.

"To tell you the truth, I didn't like his last name. I didn't know anybody whose name ended in a vowel," she laughs.

The first time Caroline saw Tom play was also Caroline's first basketball game. It was at Madison Square Garden in the National Collegiate Athletic Association (NCAA) 1952 Holiday Festival Tournament, where Tom's La Salle Explorers lost to Duquesne. At first, she wasn't a fan of the game of basketball. She would bring a book or sometimes crossword puzzles to play with if Tom wasn't in the game.

"To me, it was like watching a huge tennis match," she laughs. "Back and forth, back and forth."

She laughs about it today, but she always supported Tom throughout his career. As Tom's career developed, the crossword puzzles were no more.

In October 1954, Tom drove down to Caroline's parents' house to surprise her. He arrived at the home in Chevy Chase, Maryland, and asked Caroline's dad, Cornelius Norris, for his daughter's hand in marriage. Caroline arrived home, not knowing what was going on, and the two went for a drive near her school, Marymount College.

"He wanted to go inside at Marymount and propose to me in front of the blessed mother statue," Caroline says.

Marymount College was an all-girls school at the time, with very strict rules on men entering the campus buildings. Tom could not go inside, so he settled for another location to pop the question: Caroline's father's black Chrysler.

Eight months later, Tom and Caroline got married at the Blessed Sacrament Catholic Church in Washington, D.C., on June 25, 1955. The ceremony was a low-key event, with a small reception taking place at the Women's Club of Chevy Chase. Tom's brother John served as his best man.

7

....

Gola to the NBA

WHEN TOM GOLA started his National Basketball Association (NBA) career, the draft looked a little different than it does today. Instead of being a two-round, media-laden event broadcast around the world, the draft included fourteen rounds and a total of ninety-five picks in Gola's class. There was no NBA lottery before 1985, so teams drafted in reverse order of their records from the previous season.

There were also two picks in that draft that were known as "territorial picks." The territorial picks policy, which started in 1950 and ended in 1965, was a mechanism to help teams choose players from local colleges and universities. Each team had the right to a territorial pick in the draft. Any team with a first-round pick in the draft could forfeit its pick(s) before the draft to select any player from within a fifty-mile radius of its home arena location. In NBA history, twelve of the twenty-three players selected as territorial draft picks would later be inducted into the Naismith Memorial Basketball Hall of Fame.

That's where Gola came into play. He grew up in Philadelphia and played college basketball in Philadelphia; given his success and skill, it only made sense that the Philadelphia Warriors would make a run at the hometown kid.

"We knew we were going to get Gola," says Walt Davis, a member of the 1956 Philadelphia Warriors.

The Philadelphia Warriors had finished no better than last or second to last in the Eastern Division for the previous three years. They held the third pick in the 1955 draft, thanks to their 33–39 record in the 1954 season. The Minneapolis Lakers and the Philadelphia Warriors decided to forfeit their first-round picks to go after Dick Garmaker and Gola as their respective territorial picks. The Lakers would also forfeit their sixth overall pick, and the Warriors lost their third pick, but Gola was set to play in Philadelphia once again—this time, for the pros.

Gola wasn't the only local player to be selected in the 1955 NBA draft by the Philadelphia Warriors. Bob Schafer from Villanova was selected seventeenth overall, along with Jack Devine (selected thirty-third overall), Harry Silcox (seventh round), and Al Didriksen (eighth round).

The 1955 draft was a special year for the Big 5, as the local schools graduated six players to the pros, with four of those players being drafted by the Philadelphia Warriors. Other locals on the Warriors' veteran roster at the time included Paul Arizin, an alum of La Salle College High School, Larry Hennessy, and even former La Salle players Jack Moore and Jack George. Other notable NBA players drafted in 1955 included Maurice Stokes, Kenny Sears, Ed Conlin, Jack Twyman, and K.C. Jones.

"Everything came together, and we were local guys. We were really a local professional team. Everything fit into place," says Ernie Beck, a graduate of the University of Pennsylvania and a member of the 1955 Philadelphia Warriors.

Gola reportedly asked for a $17,500-per-year contract with the Warriors. Eddie Gottlieb, the owner of the Philadelphia Warriors, offered Gola a first-year contract worth close to $11,500.

Gola's NBA debut was far from normal. The Warriors played an exhibition game in Houlton, Maine, on October 11, 1955, against the Boston Celtics. Just two minutes into the game, Gola injured his right hand when he attempted to steal the ball from the Celtics center, Ed Macauley. Gola continued to play, although he was eventually taken out of the game.

Later that night, Gola was taken to Madigan Memorial Hospital in Houlton, where doctors told him he would need to wear a cast for up to four weeks. Dr. Eugene Gormley treated Gola's third metacarpal fracture and estimated that he possibly would be able to return to the lineup in six weeks.

Two days after the game against Boston, Gola returned to Philadelphia to be reevaluated at St. Mary's Hospital by the Phillies' then–team doctor, Thomas McTear. McTear said that there was no dislocation in the finger and that the break should hold fairly well, but Gola would remain out for three to four weeks.

The Warriors lost their season opener to the Celtics without Gola but rattled off three straight wins after the opening night loss. With the team riding a three-game winning streak, it was time for Gola to get back on the court. After the doctors cleared him to play, he made his Warriors regular-season debut on November 17, 1955, at Convention Hall against the Celtics.

Gola did not start that game against the Celtics but was substituted for George Dempsey, to roaring applause from local supporters who came to the arena to see Gola play professionally for the first time. In just twenty-four minutes of play, Gola finished the game with 10 points, 7 rebounds, and 3 assists in the 106–92 victory. His professional career was off and running.

"He was a guy, if you needed a basket or a rebound, Tommy was the guy that was there. He fit it in, and he fit it in well," says Beck.

In his first two NBA games, Gola fouled out against the Boston Celtics and the Syracuse Nationals. For the entire month of November, Gola played in seven games, five of which the Warriors won, and averaged just over 9 points a contest. In the first two months of the season, Gola was averaging more than 4 fouls a game. He played hard, but maybe a little too hard at times.

At the end of December 1955, Gola wrote an article, published in the *Philadelphia Inquirer*, titled "Gola Tells Why He Fouls as Pro." The article came just nineteen games into his professional basketball career. He opined that playing pro was a lot harder than playing college ball.

Gola told the *Philadelphia Inquirer* in 1955, "I have not been groomed to be the high scorer I was in college but instead I am to fit into a well-balanced machine doing my part as a passer, rebounder, and scorer. My biggest worry now in the switch from college to pro is the one of adjustment. I did not have any preseason training with the team so I have had to concentrate on my mates' abilities as we have played our league games. I also have a tendency to lag off defensively to help out others but this is a college zone tendency."

Gola's defensive mind-set changed from his college to pro game. The Warriors head coach, George Senesky, wanted Gola to play away from the basket. This way, Gola would have an easier one-on-one battle against his defender instead of standing closer to the rim. Although it was only a few weeks into the season, Gola and his teammates were still getting used to one another's play on the court. Gola enjoyed playing with Arizin on the give-and-go plays and Neil Johnston on the fast breaks. But his ability to score was hindered by the hand injury that he suffered in the preseason.

Gola said, "I have been hampered in the early season by the weak finger muscles due to the hand I broke in the exhibition game in Maine."

In 1956, Gola and the Warriors rode an eight-game winning streak into February, in which they averaged more than 100 points in seven of those games. The 1956 season was finished by the second week of March, with the Warriors having a 45–27 record, placing them first in the Eastern Division.

The Warriors matched up in the semifinals against the defending NBA champs, the Syracuse Nationals, a team they went 9–3 against during the regular season. In game 3 of the series against the Syracuse Nationals, the Warriors named March 27, 1956, "Tom Gola Night" at Convention Hall to honor Gola's accomplishments in Philadelphia basketball. The team had originally planned to honor Gola earlier in the season, but the plans had fallen through. Gola received a new Dodge, a gift that was in his contract prior to signing with the team, and other gifts from fans. Caroline received a new watch from New York as part of the big night. The Philadelphia Warriors won that game, 119–96, with Gola scoring 16 points. The teams split the first four games, setting up a decisive game 5 in Philadelphia. The Warriors came out on top, 109–104, led by Arizin, who scored 35 points; Gola scored 8 points in the series victory. Gola and the Warriors defeated their next opponent, the Fort Wayne Pistons, to win the NBA championship in five games, 4–1. Gola scored 69 points in the championship series but was outscored by teammate Arizin's 138 points. It was the team's first championship since 1947. In his first year in the NBA, Gola was ranked in the top five in assists per game with 5.9, with the likes of teammate Jack George, Bob Cousy (Celtics), Slater Martin (Minneapolis Lakers), and Andy Phillip (Fort Wayne Pistons).

Warriors owner Gottlieb was so confident that his team was going to finish out the championship series at home that he did not even arrange travel to Fort Wayne for game 6 of that series. His team rewarded his confidence. The Warriors celebrated heavily into the night at Sam Framo's Uptown Shrimp Emporium in Philadelphia. Gottlieb told the team that each member would get a lucrative bonus for winning the title, in addition to the $15,000 that the NBA awarded to the winning team. For the third time in four years, Gola was a champion once again—this time, an NBA champion.

"He was a reason. He *is* the reason we won the championship," Davis says. "If Tom wasn't on the team, we may have never won. We would have been a good team, but not a championship team."

Gola is one of only two players (alongside Utah Utes player Arnie Ferrin) in basketball history to win a National Invitation Tournament (NIT), a National Collegiate Athletic Association (NCAA) Tournament, and an NBA championship. Up next for Gola was a date with Uncle Sam.

8

Uncle Sam Called

O N TUESDAY, APRIL 17, 1956, just eleven days after winning the National Basketball Association (NBA) championship, Tom Gola got a phone call from the U.S. Army. A military test was waiting for him in South Philadelphia.

"I knew he was going, but I obviously didn't want him to go," Caroline says.

Ten days before this test, Gola passed a selective service physical performed by army captain Joseph Myers. In the 1950s, the U.S. military had strict guidelines regarding the height of Americans enlisting in the military: if a candidate was 6 ft. 6 in. or taller, he was too tall to serve. Gola stood 6 ft. 6 in.

"The army wanted Tom. There was no question about it," Caroline says.

Harvey Pollack, a former Philadelphia Warrior and long-time 76ers statistician, recalls taking Gola to the army test in April 1956. The Philadelphia Warriors owner, Eddie Gottlieb, was worried about the possibility of losing Gola for an extended period of time for the 1956 season. He spoke to Pollack and expressed his concerns following the team's successful championship run. Gottlieb ordered Pollack to pick up Gola at his home and take him to the U.S. Army induction center at 20th and Johnson Streets in South Philadelphia. His idea was for Gola to rest and not be on his feet prior to his testing. His hope was that if Gola stayed horizontal, he would be at his full height, but if he spent time standing, his body might settle to a height below the army's cut-off point.

"The only time he would be on his feet was when he would walk from his house to [the] car," Pollack said.

When Pollack arrived, Gola went directly to the back seat of Pollack's car, lying on his back and placing his feet over the front passenger seat. His feet were up in the air the entire ride to South Philadelphia in an effort to stretch out his body so that he would remain at his maximum height.

"That's the way I drove him. All the way from his home to the induction center," Pollack recalls.

After a twenty-minute ride to the center, Pollack told Gola to stay in the car while he went into the center to see exactly when his appointment would take place.

"Are you guys ready for Gola yet?" Pollack asked at the front desk.

The induction center was not ready. Pollack then made up a story about how Gola and Caroline were waiting in the car together to say their final good-bye, an attempt to give Gola as much time on his back as possible before his test. That story, of course, was not true, as Caroline was nowhere near South Philadelphia.

"Gola's out in the car with his wife," he said. "He just got married, and he wanted to say good-bye to his wife."

Pollack came back to the car and sat with Gola for the next twenty to twenty-five minutes. Still killing time and hoping his body would stretch a little more, Gola remained lying down in the back seat with his feet draped over the front seat. Finally, the two decided it was time to go into the center for testing.

"Yeah, they are ready for Gola now," the desk attendant said as they walked in.

Gottlieb's stretching plan lost whatever chance it had of working, as the army physicians ended up having Gola sit on a bench to wait for his turn in line. He sat there for about an hour or so, with his back curled and no structural support under his body. Finally, it was time to measure Gola and test him. Gola's height was not 6 ft. 6 in.—he was measured at 6 ft. 5¾ in. The headlines in the paper the next day read "Gola 'Shrinks' at Army Exam." His army service was automatic.

That was it for Gola's basketball career in 1956. Pollack went back to the Sheraton Hotel, the location of the Warriors main office at the time, to break the news to Gottlieb. Pollack had done all he could, but Uncle Sam got Gola.

Gola was drafted into the army on April 17, 1956, and left 30th Street Station shortly after 3:00 P.M., sporting a letterman jacket, dress pants, and dress shoes; carrying a suitcase; and waving to his family and friends who were there to say good-bye. Caroline was not at the station, because she had said good-bye to Tom right before he went for his test, intuiting that he was army-bound.

"That was like losing your right arm," Walt Davis says of losing Gola to the military. "Tom was the glue that held everyone together. Not just by his leadership qualities. It's the fact that he could do everything so good."

Davis was disappointed, as were others on the team and in the city. Yet they understood the protocol of the military's testing procedures.

"When you lose your bread and butter, . . . of course there is a disappointment," Davis says.

Gola left 30th Street Station on a 611-mile trip south to Fort Jackson in Columbia, South Carolina. Twenty-five other Philadelphia-area natives joined Gola on the trip, according to newspaper reports. Caroline could not visit Gola right away, for boot camp was strictly for the new soldiers: no family allowed.

Gola experienced a whole different lifestyle and culture in South Carolina. After six weeks at Fort Jackson, Gola was transported ninety-three miles to Fort Gordon in Augusta, Georgia, where he began work at the Signal School, learning coding in an eight-week course. Gola graduated first in his class, earning a "top secret-cryptographic" clearance. Caroline eventually moved to Georgia, where she and Gola lived in a one-bedroom army apartment complex for some time. Caroline did not have a job and enjoyed her time away from the city life. The move south was an escape from the fast pace of Philadelphia, but she recalls Georgia as being "hot as Hades." It was a fun time for Caroline, when she enjoyed some independence while Gola worked his regular army schedule.

At the apartment complex, the Golas got friendly with the Kaye family, who lived two doors down. The Kaye family had nine children living in an apartment next to them, and Caroline was even asked to become the godmother of one of the children.

Gola wanted to trade in his army khakis for his NBA uniform as soon as he could, taking advantage of the twenty-one-month rule. In the late 1950s, this rule was known to some as the "Willie Mays Rule." Baseball Hall of Famer Willie Mays was drafted into the U.S. Army in 1952 during the Korean War, missing most of the 1952 and the entire 1953 season, for a total of 266 games, due to his service. If a soldier had fulfilled his obligation after twenty-one months, he would be discharged.

On September 22, 1957, Gola was transferred to the army base at Fort Monmouth in New Jersey. Gola got the opportunity to play basketball at Fort Monmouth and even played with and against Sihugo Green from Duquesne; Green would later play nine seasons in the NBA. At Fort Monmouth, Gola's weight reached 220 pounds, and he spent his summer weekends in Wildwood, driving down the Garden State Parkway and playing basketball for fun. While Gola was in the army, some speculated that he might play with the Warriors on the weekends as long as he fulfilled his military duties first. However, this arrangement never came about. Gola, a resident of the Eatontown Estates, knew that Fort Monmouth was his last stop in his army duties, and he saved up a majority of his leave to get out of the army early. He was discharged from the army with the rank of corporal in January 1958, planning to return to the NBA.

Gola missed the entire seventy-two-game season in 1956–1957, as the Warriors lost in the Eastern Division semifinals to the Syracuse Nationals. After 581 days of not playing professional ball, Gola returned to the NBA on November 19, 1957, to face the Cincinnati Royals at home. Being drafted into the military had put Gola's professional and family life on hold for nineteen months, but he and his wife never regretted their service to their country.

"The army was good for Tom. He served his country honorably," Caroline says. "It was a big part of his life. He met a lot of interesting people and made a lot of wonderful friends. He did his job."

9

········

San Francisco and a
New York Knicks State
of Mind

I N SEPTEMBER 1958, the Warriors hired Al Cervi as their new head coach. Cervi had recently coached the Syracuse Nationals and won a National Basketball Association (NBA) championship in 1955. The Warriors finished that 1958–1959 season eight games under the .500 mark, with a 32–40 record. Tom Gola finished his first season back in Philadelphia after his service with 901 points and 710 rebounds in 64 games played. The Boston Celtics won the NBA championship in the 1958–1959 season with the help of Bob Cousy, Tom Heinsohn, K.C. Jones, and Bill Russell; coached by Arnold "Red" Auerbach, they would win eight straight NBA titles between 1959 and 1966. Bob Pettit, a power forward for the St. Louis Hawks, won the Most Valuable Player (MVP) honors, averaging 29.2 points and 16.2 rebounds per game. The 1959 NBA championship final game was the second straight meeting of the Celtics and the Hawks. In his first season in the NBA with the Philadelphia Warriors, Woody Sauldsberry from Texas Southern University won the 1958 Rookie of the Year award, the first in the team's history to win it. Gola was named to the All-NBA Second Team along with Cliff Hagan (St. Louis Hawks), Slater Martin (St. Louis Hawks), Bill Russell (MVP in 1958 with the Boston Celtics), and Maurice Stokes (Cincinnati Royals). Following the Warriors' failure to make the play-offs, Cervi resigned as their head coach.

Things seemed bleak for the Warriors, until another territorial pick changed the direction of the franchise. On March 31, 1959, the Warriors drafted Philadelphia native and Overbrook High School and University of Kansas alum Wilt Chamberlain. As one could imagine, Chamberlain's 7 ft. 1 in. height and scoring ability made an immediate impact.

The Warriors hired former player Neil Johnston to be their new head coach, just a year after his retirement in 1960. Chamberlain's presence in the NBA was felt instantly, as he scored 2,707 points and grabbed 1,941 rebounds in his first year. He won the NBA MVP and Rookie of the Year awards, thanks to having led the league in rebounding and scoring. Chamberlain averaged 37.6 points and 27 rebounds per game in the first seventy-two games of his professional career. The Warriors won forty-nine games that year, placing them second in the Eastern Conference, behind the Boston Celtics. Their season ended in the Eastern Division finals, in which the Celtics beat them four games to two.

Gola played in every game of the 1959–1960 season for the Warriors. He scored at least 15 points more than thirty-six times that year and tallied 11 triple-doubles. The 1959–1960 season, in which Gola scored 1,122 points, was his best. Gola was ranked in the top five in the NBA in assists, with 409, and in assists per game, with 5.5. For the first time in his NBA career, Gola made the All-Star Team, replacing teammate Paul Arizin, who could not play due to an injury. The 1960 All-Star game was played at Convention Hall in Philadelphia, where the East beat the West, 125–115. The East roster included Gola's teammate Chamberlain, Dolph Schayes (Syracuse Nationals), Cousy (Boston Celtics), Russell (Boston Celtics), and Richie Guerin (New York Knicks). It's not the most positive of achievements, but Gola also led the league in personal fouls, with 311.

During the off-season, on May 30, 1959, Gola and Caroline welcomed their son, Thomas Christopher Gola. Just days after celebrating the addition to their family, Gola got sick and was diagnosed with hepatitis. Caroline does not recall how her husband got the disease, but she does remember Gola's being in Hahnemann Hospital for the entire month of June. Gola was so sick that he did not attend their son's baptism. Everything was going wrong for the young family: Caroline's father, Cornelius, had suffered a fatal heart attack in April 1959, the Golas had just moved into their new house in the Bustleton section of Philadelphia, Gola was sick, and Caroline was stuck at home with no driver's license, taking care of a newborn. Gola eventually got better, but at one point during his illness, members of the Philadelphia Warriors thought that he might never be able to play again.

Just a few weeks before the start of the 1960–1961 season, the Philadelphia Warriors traded Philly-native Ernie Beck and Sauldsberry to the St. Louis Hawks for Ed Conlin and cash considerations. The Warriors added two rookies to the roster that year in guard Bill "Pickles" Kennedy from Temple University and point guard Al Attles from North Carolina Agricultural and Technical State University. The Warriors got swept in the Eastern Division semifinals by the Syracuse Nationals, thanks to the Nationals' trio of point guard Larry Costello (a teammate of Gola's in 1956), shooting guard Hal Greer, and center Schayes. (Greer and Schayes would later be inducted into the Naismith Memorial Basketball Hall of Fame.) These three players scored 190 of 336 combined points in the three-game series. After a 46–33 season with the Warriors, Johnston resigned from his coaching duties. Gola scored 10 points or more forty-nine times and scored more than 20 points eleven times during the 1961 season. For the second straight year, Gola made the All-Star Team; he would go on to make the All-Star Team five times in total during his NBA career.

Frank McGuire, from the University of North Carolina at Chapel Hill, filled the Warriors' coaching void for the 1962 season, the third coaching change in the previous four years for the franchise. McGuire had been North Carolina's men's basketball coach from 1953 to 1961 but was forced to resign when the basketball program was placed on NCAA probation in 1961. McGuire had been replaced at North Carolina by future Hall of Famer Dean Smith.

Chamberlain's dominance continued, as he averaged 50.4 points and 25.7 rebounds per game in the 1962 season. He also scored an NBA single-season record 4,029 points in eighty games. On March 2, 1962, Chamberlain scored an NBA record 100 points in a game at the Hershey Sports Arena in Hershey, Pennsylvania. In *Wilt, 1962*, author Gary Pomerantz reveals that Gola, nursing an injury, was listening to the game in Philadelphia at a neighbor's house on WCAU radio, with announcer Bill Campbell calling the game. The game in Hershey was not televised.

"[Gola] was injured and didn't play. Wilt would have still gotten 100 points regardless of who played," laughs Attles, a Philadelphia Warrior.

Dave Zinkoff was the public address announcer for the Philadelphia Warriors in 1962 and called Chamberlain's 100-point game in Hershey.

Zinkoff had attended Central High School in Philadelphia and graduated from Temple University in 1932. He worked for the Phillies at Shibe Park, worked at the old Philadelphia Convention Hall, and announced other wrestling and boxing events. He was known for his colorful public introductions of players before and during the games. Fans enjoyed hearing witty phrases from Zinkoff, such as when he announced "Dipper Dunk!" after a Chamberlain basket. Zinkoff's unique announcing career started at the Palestra when Gola played in the 1950s.

"It all started with Tom Gola," Zinkoff said to *Sports Illustrated* in 1984. "I was doing the doubleheaders at the Palestra, always shouting, 'Field goal Gola, field goal Gola.' Soon it became 'Gola goal,' and everybody loved it."

The Warriors lost to the Boston Celtics in the Eastern Division finals that season, four games to three. Gola averaged 13.7 points and 9.8 rebounds in sixty games played. He was the third-best scorer on the team, behind Chamberlain and Arizin.

In May 1962, the Warriors owner, Eddie Gottlieb, asked the NBA directors for approval to sell the team. The sale would move the team 2,875 miles west to San Francisco. Three weeks after this meeting with the NBA directors, the team was officially sold, moving on May 23, 1962. The team was sold for $850,000 to Matty Simmons and Leonard Mogel, both from New York. Bernard Solomon was also involved in the acquisition of the Warriors and was reportedly the head of the group obtaining the team. The radio and television producer Franklin Mieuli became the majority owner. From 1962 to 1964 and from 1966 to 1971, the San Francisco Warriors played their home games at the Cow Palace in Daly City, California. The San Francisco Warriors would change their name to the Golden State Warriors for the 1971–1972 season. Mieuli would sell the Warriors in 1986.

At the time of the sale, only the Celtics and the Knicks voted against the Warriors' move to San Francisco. Both teams wanted the Warriors to stay in Philadelphia with the idea that the franchises could play more games against each other. More local rivalry games between the three teams would be a lucrative box office magnet. From 1960 to 1962, the Warriors played the Knicks a total of twenty-five times and the Celtics a total of twenty-six times.

After selling the Warriors, Gottlieb was reportedly going to organize a new team in Philadelphia that would be strictly built on local talent. Maurice Podoloff, the NBA president at the time, indicated that a new team would indeed go to Philadelphia. Gottlieb was also rumored to be interested in purchasing the Detroit Pistons and the Chicago Packers to replace the Warriors. Gottlieb also bid on the Syracuse Nationals but was turned down. The Syracuse Nationals were purchased by Philadelphians Isadore "Irv" Kosloff and Ike Richman in the spring of 1963. The NBA approved the franchise shift and the name change from the Nationals to the Philadelphia 76ers.

The 1962 Warriors included four players from Big 5 schools and Conlin, who had attended Fordham in the Bronx, in New York. Staying close to home was important to Arizin and Gola; they both wanted to stay on the East Coast.

"He was a Philadelphia person. East Coast was East Coast. He wanted to stay home," Caroline says.

In July 1962, Gola approached Vince McNally, then the Philadelphia Eagles general manager, about the possibility of switching sports from basketball to football. Gola was upset about the move and the sale of the Philadelphia Warriors, and he wanted to find alternatives to stay closer to his family. Gola did not like the fact that he would be playing 2,800 miles away from family and friends for more than six months. Gola, who was twenty-eight years old at the time of the tryout with the Eagles, weighed close to 220 pounds. The last time Gola had played football was back at La Salle College High School during his freshman and sophomore years; he had quit the sport to concentrate on basketball after suffering a shoulder injury. Even though Gola was strong and tall, he did not have what it took to be hit every day in Eagles practice. Gola never signed a contract with the Eagles, instead continuing to play for the Warriors.

"I found I wasn't prepared physically to go through with it," Gola told the *Philadelphia Inquirer* in July 1962. "All of the Eagles are big boys and they're in the peak of condition for football."

Gola made it known that if the Eagles tryout was unsuccessful, he would want to play for the Knicks in New York.

"I think if I had started to get in shape six weeks ago, I'd have been able to make a go of it, but under the circumstances I think it's best that we drop the whole thing," Gola said in the same *Inquirer* article.

Gola, Caroline, and their young son, Thomas Christopher, made the ten-day drive to San Francisco. The move to the West Coast was tough for everyone involved, but especially Gola's wife, Caroline.

"It was kind of a cross-the-country-like-the-Griswolds thing," Thomas says. Not that the family saw it this way at the time: *National Lampoon's Vacation* wouldn't be released until 1983.

The Golas struggled to find a place to live in their first months in San Francisco, because no apartment complex at the time would take a child. Caroline recalls that they would take a dog, but "we couldn't find a place that could take a child."

As a young mother, Caroline was frustrated by the difficulty of trying to make her family comfortable in a new city they knew nothing about. Luckily, one of the Warriors front office workers found the family a luxurious apartment in the Nob Hill neighborhood of San Francisco. Caroline recalls that the massive apartment boasted a fireplace, close proximity to the InterContinental Mark Hopkins Hotel, and a spectacular view of Alcatraz Island. They paid close to $700 a month in rent to live there. But as the 1962 NBA season began, Caroline's emotions were getting the best of her on the West Coast.

"I told Tom this was not working. I want[ed] to go home," she says.

A Warriors front office staff member came over to the Golas' apartment one day to talk to the family about Gola's future with the team out west. The Warriors gave Gola the option of not being traded, but the family decided it was for the best to find a way back to the East Coast.

"Tom was a city boy. A hometown boy. That's the way he was," Caroline says.

The Warriors got on the phone with the New York Knicks, and on December 5, 1962, Gola was traded to the Knicks for Kenny Sears and Willie Naulls. Naulls had led the Knicks in rebounding four of his last six seasons with the team, and Sears had been a first-round draft pick. The Knicks were 12.5 games out of first place at the time and were looking for a scoring punch. At the time, the Warriors were in third place in the Western Division, 9.5 games out of first place.

"I wouldn't have gone there [to San Francisco] in the first place. I've always liked playing in New York. I had hoped to be there [New York] from the start of the season," Gola told the *Philadelphia Inquirer* a day after the trade.

The trade was a homecoming for Sears, too, as he reunited with his former college coach at Santa Clara, Bob Feerick, who was in his first year at the helm of the new Warriors team.

"I was happy [to be traded], because I was very unhappy in New York," Sears says. "We were on a losing team. I didn't think I was being appreciated at all."

Sears's hometown of Watsonville, California, is a ninety-mile drive from San Francisco. Reuniting with Feerick made the trade to the Warriors even sweeter.

"I was delighted to go to San Francisco, because, number one, my old coach—who I was very fond of—we had a very good relationship," Sears says.

The Warriors gave Gola the option to stay with the team out west, but the deal was a perfect opportunity to go home to the Somerton section of Philadelphia. Gola was New York bound, ready to join a losing team with an 8–19 record under its second-year head coach, Eddie Donovan.

"We welcomed him. We were struggling to win a few games, and he came up and made some contributions. When a team is not doing so well, they make changes," recalls Johnny Green, a member of the 1962 New York Knicks.

Green had started his career with the Knicks in 1959, being selected fifth overall in the first round of the draft.

"Gola was a very likable person. It made it easy for him to come and mesh with the team," Green says. "It takes a while to get used to playing with your new teammates, or maybe the system is different. It's a number of things. I'm sure, emotionally, instincts come into play. It affects people differently."

The Knicks were entering their third season with a losing record and had gone through three coaching changes in three years, from Andrew "Fuzzy" Levane to Carl Braun to Donovan.

"It's a lot of uncertainty and frustration. When you're losing, there's a certain amount of unhappiness that comes with that. When a player comes in and [is] put into a situation like that, it's kind of a lot of responsibility. Anyone would want to come in and become the savior. There was a lot of turmoil during that time. Gola handled it very well," Green says.

Gola averaged 13 points and 7 rebounds per game in the twenty-one he played with the San Francisco Warriors before his trade. The Warriors were riding an eight-game losing streak just as Gola left. In his debut for the Knicks, Gola scored 19 points in a 99–96 victory over the Cincinnati Royals.

With the Knicks, Gola got more opportunities to score easily. Gola played thirty games in front of the home crowd at Madison Square Garden, where he averaged 10.9 points per game. Coach Donavan consistently toggled Gola's positions between forward and guard.

Gola told the *Philadelphia Bulletin* in 1965, "If I were beginning instead of drawing close to the end of my career[,] I think I'd pay far more attention to shooting. It's of paramount importance today."

New York Knicks forward Dave Budd had first met Gola during the 1960 season. Gola's leadership was what the Knicks needed at the time of the trade to turn things around.

"We got a veteran who was fundamentally [as] sound as anybody," Budd says.

Gola and Budd became close friends while playing together in New York. The two commuted together to and from practices and games in New York City. Budd lived in Woodbury, New Jersey, at the time and would meet Gola at Exit 7 on the New Jersey Turnpike to pick him up. The pair would ride in Budd's gold 1963 Chevy Super Sport for the ninety-minute commute. If Budd couldn't take Gola, Caroline would drive her husband to the Trenton train station around 4:00 P.M. for his 8:00 P.M. games. Budd remembers Gola's talking about the 1955 National Collegiate Athletic Association (NCAA) championship year quite frequently during their long drives.

"I don't think he ever got over losing the championship to [Bill] Russell. But if you got to lose, it's not too bad of a guy to lose to," Budd says.

Budd remembers traveling up to New England with Gola to participate in summer camps and to promote basketball throughout the surrounding New York region.

"He was all about team first," Budd says.

Gola had a team of his own that would come up to New York to visit and watch him play every Thursday during doubleheaders at the old Madison Square Garden: Gola's brother Paul and friends Joe Malizia and Gus Chialastri.

"It was like he worked at New York and would come home at night," Caroline says.

Prior to the games, Mo, Joe, and Gus would get large sandwiches at a New York delicatessen or eat at a local Italian restaurant. Gola would always pay the bill. After the day's doubleheader, Gola and his crew would linger in the Knicks' locker room. Gola was a little slower than some of the other guys getting ready to leave, and, of course, beer was always a selection of choice in the locker room after a game. Gola and the crew would throw the beers into a duffle bag and head back to Philly.

"They would come home reeking of garlic," Caroline laughs.

The four of them would bring back corned beef sandwiches, shrimp salads, a cup of tea, and even some New York cheesecake from the trip to New York City. Mo would drive back, while the other guys enjoyed a beer or two on the ride home. Mo would have to get up early the next day to teach American government at Father Judge High School in Northeast Philadelphia. The crew would get home around 1:00 or 2:00 A.M. Mo would get up at five, eat a little breakfast, and head to work. These weekly New York visits with his brother and friends were incorporated into his lesson plans.

"Needless to say, Fridays were a special day of films and class discussion," Mo recalls. "I programmed my lesson plan that way."

Just twenty-three days after being traded, Gola faced his old Warriors squad at Madison Square Garden. He scored only 6 points in the 114–109 loss. Gola ended up playing the Warriors five times that season, with two of those games being back in Philly. Gola's best game against the Warriors was 16 points in a win for the Knicks, on February 22, 1963.

Gola played fifty-two games with the Knicks during the remainder of the 1962 season. Of those games, the Knicks lost thirty-eight, including a ten-game losing streak to finish the year. They finished fourth in the NBA Eastern Division with an NBA worst record of 21–59, but Gola was named to the All-Star Game in 1962. However, he did not play due to an injury and was replaced by Johnny Green of the Knicks. Gola would make the All-Star Team each year from 1960 to 1964.

Gola ended up playing four total seasons with the Knicks, over 277 games. Some of those games were coached by Harry Gallatin, the man who replaced Donovan when he was fired in 1965.

"He was a versatile type of player. He is good, as he is defensive as he was offensive. He had a really good idea of how the game should be played. He is one of the best all-around players to play in the NBA," Gallatin says.

Gallatin coached the Knicks for only twenty-one games in 1965 before getting fired at the end of November, to be replaced by Dick McGuire. McGuire had been a player-coach for the Detroit Pistons in 1959–1960 and had coached the team until 1963. Len Chappell, a former Knicks teammate, recalls his brief playing time with Gola in New York.

"He was a great player. He epitomizes everything you would want in a teammate," Chappell says. "He played the game the way it should have been played."

In his second year in the league, the 1965–1966 season, Knicks point guard Emmette Bryant looked up to Gola for his leadership. Bryant had grown up reading about Gola in magazines during his days at DePaul University and had admired how stylishly Gola presented himself off the court.

"He had the sort of politician persona about him. He was smooth. Always dressed nicely with a tie on all the time. While we were wearing turtlenecks and bell-bottoms and stuff. He had that aura about him. He had that statesmanship," Bryant says.

Bryant remembers Gola's arriving to Knicks practices carrying a briefcase and looking dapper.

"He had the look of always coming to work with a briefcase and looking very lawyerish," Bryant recalls.

Gola was close to the end of his NBA career, so he wasn't reluctant to impart wisdom from his tenure in the league.

"He knew he was at the end of his time. He was gracious enough to share information and things that would help me become a better player and in turn would help the team," Bryant says. "He mentored me, and I am very appreciative of that."

Gola's playing time on the court was dwindling. He played in seventy-four games in the 1965–1966 season and averaged only 4.4 points per game, his lowest scoring average of his professional career. The writing was on the wall for Gola to hang up his shorts for good.

Gola's last game in Philadelphia was on March 18, 1966, against the Philadelphia 76ers, where the Knicks lost, 115–106, and he scored 2 points. Convention Hall in Philadelphia was packed with Gola supporters, and more than 150 young Republicans from the Sixty-Third Ward came to kick off his political campaign. People held placards reading, "Gola Victory," "63rd Ward for Gola," "Tom Will Win Again," "I'm a Nobody for Tom Gola," and "I'm for Tom and He's for Us." People believed that Gola was going to become a politician and that the groundwork for his future campaign was just starting. He was going to trade in his jersey and shorts for a red tie and a suit.

"I think the early years are the most exciting of a man's career," Gola said. "As the years go on, it becomes a job. Mentally it's tougher than physically. You can go out there and run around, but you don't get up for a game like you used to."

After four seasons with the Knicks, Gola's career ended in 1966, with his last game on March 22, 1966, against the St. Louis Hawks. In seven seasons in the NBA, Gola played 698 games (277 with the New York Knicks), scored 7,871 points, and snagged 5,617 rebounds. Gola's NBA career on paper was a lot different from his days playing at La Salle. Gola did win an NBA title, but for the first time in his playing career, Gola played against other superstars in the league, and the talent discrepancy leveled out. Gola's basketball playing days were over. He was onto his next adventure: politics.

10

....

The "Behind the Iron Curtain" Tour

IN THE SPRING OF 1964, Nick Rodis, the chairman of the U.S. State Department's Agency on International Athletics, called the Boston Celtics' head coach, Arnold "Red" Auerbach, and asked him to form a team to travel across the Atlantic for a basketball event to later be called the "Behind the Iron Curtain" tour. The U.S. squad would play against other countries' top basketball players in Poland, Romania, Egypt, and Yugoslavia. The main message of the excursion was to promote the style of American basketball and to demonstrate the fundamentals of the game. In so doing, the State Department hoped to get the international community hooked on an appealing aspect of American culture in the midst of the Cold War. Auerbach selected Bill Russell, Tom Heinsohn, K.C. Jones, and Bob Cousy from the Boston Celtics; Jerry Lucas and Oscar Robertson from the Cincinnati Royals; Bob Pettit from the St. Louis Hawks; and Tom Gola from the New York Knicks. (Each of these players would be inducted into the Naismith Memorial Basketball Hall of Fame.)

"We helped spread the word about basketball. We were kind of the floor runners. We did it with our best players," says long-time Boston Celtic Cousy.

Prior to leaving the United States, the team, trainers, and coaches had a briefing meeting with Dean Rusk, then the secretary of state, at the nation's capital to discuss how the team would handle the tense relationships overseas during the height of the Cold War. The State Department stressed to the National Basketball Association (NBA) players the importance of patience when communicating with other countries' players and their political leaders. The eight team members met with President Lyndon B. Johnson in the Oval Office before their departure, when he encouraged the team to do their best in representing America. The NBA season ended in April 1964, and the team left in May to launch the "Behind the Iron Curtain" Tour. The name of the tour referred to the separation of two areas in Europe—one capitalist and one Communist—that defined global politics at the close of World War II and the beginning of the Cold War.

The U.S. team started the trip in Warsaw, Poland, without Coach Auerbach, who was back in the United States working on the upcoming NBA draft. Cousy coached the first two games for the team, which they won by more than 20 points each. The United States faced Poland five times during their time in Warsaw.

"No one tested us in any way," Cousy says.

Boston Celtic Tom Heinsohn wrote for the *Boston Globe* during the tour and wired the articles back to the United States. Heinsohn was known as the team's troublemaker, because he was always causing a stir on and off the court. During some down time in Krakow, Poland, the group participated in a tour of the German concentration camps at Auschwitz. During the visit, the U.S. team members flipped the tables and caused Heinsohn some discomfort. They pointed to Heinsohn, yelling the word, "Deutsch! Deutsch!" Germans were not popular in postwar Poland.

Auerbach and others on the team continued to prank Heinsohn during their stay in Poland. Gola, Lucas, and Heinsohn were roommates living in a suite. During one prank, Gola was shaving in the bathroom of the suite, and Heinsohn was writing an article for the *Boston Globe*. The group heard a knock at their door, and Heinsohn opened the door to see two tall men in white raincoats.

"Heinsohn!" one man said. "Get the passport and come with us."

Auerbach and Cousy had arranged for two men to dress up in trench coats and demand Heinsohn's personal information. The team was on high alert the entire trip because the State Department had told the team that it was possible that police from each country would be listening in on their trip.

Heinsohn went with the two men, who were actually former members of the Polish national basketball team. The two tall men argued in Polish with each other as they walked Heinsohn out of the hotel and into a dark alley.

"I thought they were gonna shoot me!" Heinsohn recalls.

The prank ended as Heinsohn was taken into a small dark room, where some of his laughing teammates surprised him.

"That prank was one of the best ever!" Lucas says. "It turned out to be one of the biggest and best pranks in history for all I'm concerned. I was scared to death."

Heinsohn decided to get even with some of the players who pranked him. He set up a plan to get Gola back for participating.

Gola always traveled with a camera to capture the moments of the trip. While at the pool in Cairo, Egypt, Heinsohn decided to take Gola's camera and take some photos.

"Every bikini that was there got the full treatment with the zoom lens. From top to bottom," Heinsohn says.

He shot a lot of camera footage that afternoon at the pool to get back at Gola.

"I got him for the arrest in Poland!" Heinsohn says.

The following season, Gola and Heinsohn were slated to play against each other. In the days before the game, Gola had shown his family some of the photos from the trip. The photos that Heinsohn took came up, catching Gola completely unaware. At the first game of the season, Gola punched Heinsohn in the gut as soon as the ball went up.

The "Behind the Iron Curtain" team made stops in the former Yugoslavia, including at the now-capital of Croatia, Zagreb. The U.S. team played against the Yugoslavian national team in an outdoor soccer stadium with thousands in attendance. Before one of the games, stadium officials did not fly the American flag, nor were they planning on playing the U.S. national anthem. Auerbach pulled his team off the court and refused to play until they played the national anthem. After a brief delay and confrontation between Auerbach and stadium officials, the U.S. flag was raised, and the national anthem was played. The U.S. team won that game against Yugoslavia by 32 points.

At the start of the second game against Yugoslavia, Russell tipped the opening toss to Heinsohn, who drove to the basket for an easy lay-up. On his drive to the basket, Heinsohn got hit by a Yugoslavian player's fist, which knocked both of them to the ground.

"I think we all were a little concerned right when things were happening," Lucas recalls.

Lucas says he was told that the other team was embarrassed from their loss in the first night's game, and the rough play was some sort of retaliation against the Americans. The tour was not in danger of ending, but the games were filled with animosity.

"It became a political thing," Cousy says.

The "Behind the Iron Curtain" team played a total of nineteen games. The trip was a special opportunity for the NBA players to experience basketball overseas, but for Pettit, the trip created some closer friendships with players he played against in the NBA.

"In my era of basketball, there were very few guys that you played against that you became really friendly with," Pettit says. "I felt I became a good friend to Tom. I didn't say that for many players that I played against."

Cousy enjoyed the "Behind the Iron Curtain" trip and further enjoyed playing with and against Gola during his NBA tenure.

"Despite his successful career, in the minds of a lot of fans, I thought he was underrated. He was an outstanding [player] without being flashy," Cousy says. "He didn't score that much because he was surrounded by some scorers. He didn't get the attention in my judgment that he probably deserved."

The "Behind the Iron Curtain" team returned to the United States in June 1964. The players never lost a basketball game overseas.

From 1952 to 1955, Tom Gola scored 2,462 points and collected 2,201 rebounds. Gola and Joe Holup (George Washington University) are the only players in National Collegiate Athletic Association (NCAA) history to have scored more than 2,000 points and collected 2,000 rebounds. *(La Salle University Archives.)*

La Salle compiled a 102–19 record during Gola's playing career. *(La Salle University Archives.)*

Ken Loeffler, who coached La Salle's Explorers from 1949 to 1955, took the team to six major postseason tournaments—most notably to the National Invitation Tournament (NIT) championship in 1952, to the NCAA championship in 1954, and to NCAA runner-up status in 1955. *(La Salle University Archives.)*

In Gola's freshman year at La Salle, the Explorers won the 1952 NIT championship. The following season, the team lost to St. John's in the quarterfinals of the NIT. *(La Salle University Archives.)*

Gola poses with La Salle Explorer teammates: Bob Maples, Frank Blatcher (to Gola's left), and Fran O'Malley (to Gola's right). *(La Salle University Archives.)*

Shown here are the 1954 NCAA champion La Salle Explorers: *Front row (left to right):* Frank Blatcher, Bob Maples, Frank O'Hara, Tom Gola, and Bob Ames. *Back row (left to right):* Charles Greenberg, Fran O'Malley, Manuel Gomez, John Yodsnukis, Charles Singley, and John Moosbrugger. *(La Salle University Archives.)*

The 1954 La Salle Explorers were inducted into the La Salle Hall of Athletics in 1984. The 1954 championship team went 26–4 and was ranked second behind Kentucky in the 1954 Associated Press (AP) national poll. *(La Salle University Archives.)*

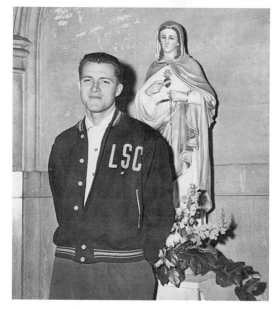

Gola served as La Salle's team captain in 1954 and 1955. He went on to become a four-time All-American and a three-time consensus All-American. *(La Salle University Archives.)*

Josh Cody, Temple University's director of athletics, presents the Robert V. Geasey Trophy to La Salle's captain and All-American, Tom Gola, following the city college basketball championship at Convention Hall in Philadelphia, where the Explorers defeated Temple, 59–57, in overtime.

(From the Philadelphia Evening Bulletin *Photograph Collection. Courtesy of the Special Collections Research Center, Temple University Libraries, Philadelphia, PA.)*

The La Salle Explorers
faced the West Virginia
Mountaineers in the 1955
NCAA Tournament and won,
95–61. Gola scored 22 points
and grabbed 16 rebounds.
(From the Philadelphia Evening
Bulletin *Photograph Collection.*
Courtesy of the Special Collections
Research Center, Temple University
Libraries, Philadelphia, PA.)

Gola holds an NCAA
record for accumulating 48
straight double-doubles from
December 2, 1953, to January
29, 1955, and an NCAA
record for accumulating 96
double-doubles during his
tenure. *(La Salle University
Archives.)*

Gola ranks third in La Salle's all-time scoring, behind Michael Brooks (2,628 points) and Lionel Simmons (3,217 points). *(La Salle University Archives.)*

Shown here is the 1955 NCAA runner-up team: *Front row (left to right):* Charles Singley, Bob Maples, Fran O'Malley, Alonzo Lewis, and Joe Gilson. *Middle row (left to right):* Mario Vetere (trainer), Manuel Gomez, Tom Gola, John Yodsnukis, Walt Fredericks, and Ken Loeffler (coach). *Back row (left to right):* Bill Bickley, Bob Ames, John Gola, Charles Greenberg, Bob Kraemer, Frank Blatcher, and Leo Murphy (manager). *(La Salle University Archives.)*

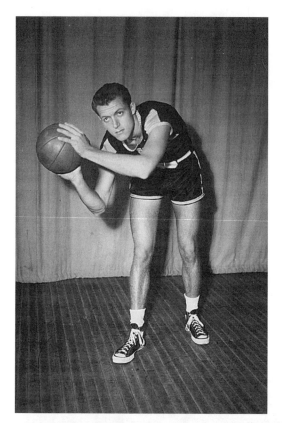

Gola is currently the all-time four-year NCAA rebound leader, with 2,201. He averaged 19 rebounds per game during his tenure at 20th and Olney. *(La Salle University Archives.)*

Gola, being examined here by Captain Joseph H. Myers at Schuylkill Arsenal in Philadelphia, passed the selective service examination in April 1956. *(From the Philadelphia Evening Bulletin Photograph Collection. Courtesy of the Special Collections Research Center, Temple University Libraries, Philadelphia, PA.)*

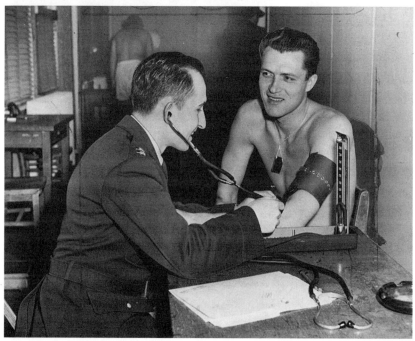

Playing for the New York Knicks, Gola blocks a shot by Philadelphia 76er Wilt Chamberlain at Philadelphia's Convention Hall in March 1965. Gola, a close friend of Chamberlain's, spoke at his funeral in 1999. *(From the* Philadelphia Evening Bulletin *Photograph Collection. Courtesy of the Special Collections Research Center, Temple University Libraries, Philadelphia, PA.)*

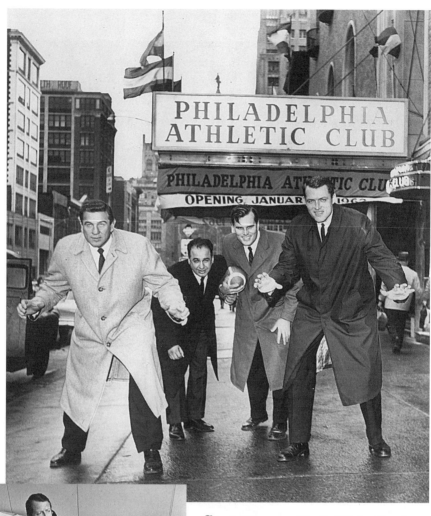

Chuck "Concrete Charlie" Bednarik, of the Philadelphia Eagles; Frank Novick, the vice president of the Philadelphia Athletic Club; John B. Kelly Jr., the president of the Philadelphia Athletic Club; and Gola, of the Philadelphia Warriors, pose playfully in front of the club in January 1962. *(From the* Philadelphia Evening Bulletin *Photograph Collection. Courtesy of the Special Collections Research Center, Temple University Libraries, Philadelphia, PA.)*

Gola was elected to two terms as a member of the Pennsylvania State Legislature, in 1966 and 1968, and he was elected Philadelphia city controller in 1969. *(La Salle University Archives.)*

Gola speaks as the new basketball coach for La Salle College at his introductory press conference in 1968. Under Gola's two-season leadership, the Explorers went 37–13. *(La Salle University Archives.)*

Gola shakes hands with Brother Daniel Bernian, the president of La Salle College (1958–1969), in 1968, while Jim Henry, the director of La Salle athletics, looks on. *(La Salle University Archives.)*

In his first year as the head coach for La Salle, Gola led the Explorers to a 23–1 season. He was named the 1969 National Coach of the Year by New York and Philadelphia Sports Writers. *(La Salle University Archives.)*

In the 1968–1969 season, the Explorers' only loss was to the South Carolina Gamecocks in the Quaker City Tournament at the Spectrum in Philadelphia. *(La Salle University Archives.)*

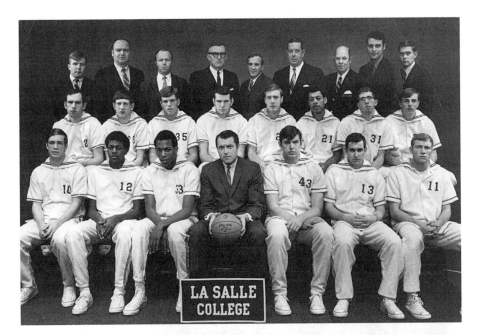

The 1968–1969 La Salle men's basketball team reached as high as second in the national polls and was inducted into the Philadelphia Big 5 Hall of Fame in 2016. (*La Salle University Archives.*)

Gola—who averaged 11.3 points and 8 rebounds in ten NBA seasons and played in four NBA All-Star games and thirty-nine playoff games, compiling regular-season totals of 7,871 points, 5,605 rebounds, and 2,953 assists—won the hearts of fans of all ages. (*La Salle University Archives.*)

Gola, La Salle's head basketball coach, with co-captains Fran Dunphy (left) and Ken Durrett (right). *(From the* Philadelphia Evening Bulletin *Photograph Collection. Courtesy of the Special Collections Research Center, Temple University Libraries, Philadelphia, PA.)*

Gola stands smiling behind Arlen Specter at the Sheraton Hotel on election night in November 1969. *(From the* Philadelphia Evening Bulletin *Photograph Collection. Courtesy of the Special Collections Research Center, Temple University Libraries, Philadelphia, PA.)*

Gola poses outside the Tom Gola Arena at the Hayman Center on the campus of La Salle University. The Pennsylvania State Assembly named November 21, 1998, "Tom Gola Day" in honor of the arena's dedication. *(La Salle University Archives.)*

Gola gives a heartfelt speech to a sold-out crowd at the Tom Gola Arena dedication. *(La Salle University Archives.)*

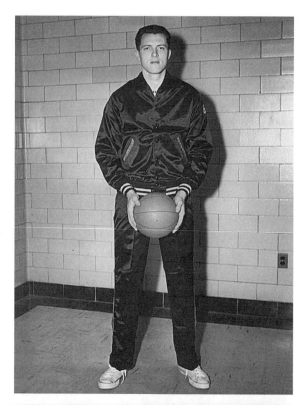

Gola was inducted into the basketball Hall of Fame in Springfield, Massachusetts, in 1975. *(La Salle University Archives.)*

Gola is a member of the Helms College Basketball Hall of Fame, the Pennsylvania Sports Hall of Fame, the Philadelphia Sports Hall of Fame, and the Madison Square Garden Hall of Fame. *(La Salle University Archives.)*

11

....

Gola Becomes Head Coach
at La Salle

ROLAND "FATTY" TAYLOR had to get out of the Northeast projects of Washington, D.C. He didn't know how or when, but if he didn't leave, he knew he might end up six feet under. Too many of his friends were either getting killed, stealing, or hopping in and out of jail.

"I wanted to change my life around, but I had to get out of D.C.," Taylor says.

Taylor attended Joel Elias Spingarn Senior High School, in the Carver Langston neighborhood of Washington, D.C. Taylor often got into fights during this time. With just one year left in high school, Taylor needed a change, so he decided to attend Fairmont Heights High School in Maryland for his senior year.

"I had to change my lifestyle," he says.

At Fairmont Heights, Taylor played baseball, football, and basketball. His play was getting noticed by college recruiters, but his grades were not good enough to receive scholarships to most schools.

Taylor's journey to Philadelphia started in a barbershop in August 1965, when he saw an ad for Dodge City Community College in a magazine.

"I said, 'That's where I want to go,'" Taylor recalls.

Taylor researched the school, which is located in Dodge City, Kansas, and wrote the head basketball coach a letter asking for a tryout for the basketball team. The head coach replied with a scholarship offer and a spot on the team.

Taylor had paved his way out of Washington, D.C., for another new opportunity. Moving to the Midwest was an adjustment for him after growing up in an African American community on the East Coast. His mother, Viola Taylor, did not have much in her pocket to help support this move, but she did offer her son some advice.

"My mom said she had no money to give me, but she would give me some words of wisdom: 'Go out there and do your best,'" Taylor says.

With a tightly wrapped lunch made by his mother, on August 25, 1965, Taylor made the journey to Dodge City, Kansas.

"I was determined that I would change my life around," Taylor says.

Taylor immediately saw playing time at Dodge City Community College. During a thirty-two-team junior college tournament in Hudson, Kansas, he met Jim Harding, then La Salle's head coach. Harding spoke with Taylor and showed him a brochure for La Salle that included a photo of Bernie Williams. That familiar face was all the convincing Taylor needed to head back east to join the 1968 La Salle team.

"I [had] always admired him [Williams] when I saw him on the playground," Taylor says.

Taylor and Williams were both from Washington, D.C., but grew up in different neighborhoods. Taylor admired Williams's play on the court.

"I went to La Salle because of Bernie Williams," Taylor says.

Harding lasted only one year as La Salle's head coach. Harding took the Explorers to the first round of the National Collegiate Athletic Association (NCAA) Tournament in 1968, but they lost to Columbia, 83–69, in College Park, Maryland. Harding's 1967–1968 team had La Salle's first twenty-win season since 1954, when Tom Gola had led the Explorers to the NCAA title.

"Jim's way was difficult for us to handle. We were out there for hours and hours and hours. He was very tough on you, but he was a fabulous teacher of the game of basketball. He had all of that down perfectly. He was tough, and he was hard on you. None of us [had] ever been through any of that," recalls Fran Dunphy, a La Salle player under Harding.

Players from Harding's 1967–1968 team perceived him as strict. Harding was a detail-oriented coach who was hard on his players. His coaching habits reflected a Jekyll-and-Hyde quality.

"It was a military practice. It was pretty rough," says Bill Michuda, a member of the La Salle team.

None of the La Salle players had previously experienced a hard coaching style like Harding brought to the team. He meant well, but his teaching habits were strict.

"If the WWE [World Wrestling Entertainment] had been as popular then, Jim Harding would have been the perfect Sgt. Slaughter. He was a tyrant. He was a bully. He was one of those 'my way or the highway' type of guys," notes Frank Bilovsky, a long-time *Philadelphia Bulletin* writer.

Stan Wlodarczyk, who was a senior heading into the 1969 season, debated whether to return to La Salle for his final year. Coach Harding was taking the fun out of the game of basketball for the Mahanoy, Pennsylvania, native.

"I wasn't actually sure if I was going to come back my senior year. I would have stayed at the school, but depending on who the coach was actually going to be determined whether or not I was going to play my senior year. That's how much he [Harding] had taken the game away from me. It was a business. It was a job. It was no fun anymore," Wlodarczyk says.

In October 1968, the NCAA brought the hammer down on La Salle's basketball program and Athletic Department, not because of Harding's practices but because of improper monetary payments to players. An eighteen-member NCAA committee censured La Salle College, St. Bonaventure, and Florida State, placing them on probation for rules infractions and violations of their respective basketball programs. The NCAA met over a three-day span in St. Louis to discuss the proper penalties for the three teams. St. Bonaventure had expensed a trip for a baseball recruit to a basketball tournament that was near the recruit's home or the university's campus. The Florida State basketball program had organized and conducted drills and practice sessions for prospective athletic scholarship winners. Florida State had also provided a free sightseeing trip to Panama City, Florida, for two recruits visiting the campus, and the team had held organized summer practices with the coaches in attendance.

Arthur Bergstrom, the NCAA's assistant director, placed St. Bonaventure and Florida State on a one-year probation that banned them from all basketball activities. However, La Salle's punishment was a two-year playoff probation.

In 1965, A to C House Cleaning Service, located in Media, Pennsylvania, was one place where La Salle students could do their work-study program to help with finances during school. According to their agreement with La Salle, A to C House Cleaning Service paid six La Salle student athletes—four basketball players and two swimmers—over a lengthy period for work that they didn't complete or for which they had falsified time cards. The four basketball players were Larry Cannon, Williams, Wlodarczyk, and Ken Durrett; the two swimmers were Bill Pleas and Jay Tract. One player was said to have received $15.01 a week, and another had received $12.53 per week, while the remaining four players had each received $10.10 a week.

"I wasn't stunned by the amount of money it was. It was an amenity almost," says Michuda.

Cannon recalls that the players actually did report to work at A to C House Cleaning Service but were told that their services were not needed.

"It was stupid. It was silly that they didn't know enough to just hand us the $15 or $20 a week or whatever it was in cash. It was just too stupid," he says.

Cannon believes that the money given to players did not hurt anyone or the program.

"It's still a controversy. The whole NCAA thing. It's . . . eighteen- and twenty-year-old kids who are on college campuses, who have no means of putting some change in their pocket," he says. "It didn't help much. It was change. It was gas money. It was nothing. It was miscellaneous money. They weren't handing us $1,000 a week. It was a couple of dollars."

A to C House Cleaning Service was owned and operated by 1940 La Salle alum Frank Loughney, who had been an All-American on the 1939 Explorers basketball team. Loughney had been drafted by the San Diego Clippers in July 1940, a month after his graduation from La Salle.

Tired of personality conflicts, head coach Harding had also tried to take away Fran Scott's basketball scholarship during the 1967 season, which was a violation of the NCAA guidelines. Scott had been unhappy at La Salle and had concerns regarding where the program was headed; he would later quit the team. After Harding left La Salle, Scott's scholarship was restored by order of the NCAA. Harding's wrongdoing had been discovered by the long-time *Philadelphia Inquirer* columnist Frank Dolson. Dolson had investigated the La Salle basketball program and reported his findings to the NCAA.

The NCAA also stated that La Salle had violated another rule when a coach of the freshman basketball team had operated an incentive system, giving out payments of about 25 cents to his players for outstanding performances. The NCAA counsel also reported that a La Salle coach had advised at least one student on the team to withhold information while being interviewed by a member of the NCAA committee. La Salle fans were disappointed as, yet again, the team would have to search for another head coach. The 1968 season would be the third consecutive year in which the Explorers had a different head coach for their home opener. La Salle did not have to go far for their next head coach: the school looked no further than Tom Gola.

"We heard that Bobby Knight was going to come. We all said if Bobby Knight is coming, we are all going to quit. We just went through Harding—we didn't need Bobby Knight next. That's what the rumor was going around," recalls La Salle player Ed Szczesny.

In August 1968, the thirty-five-year-old Gola was introduced as the new head basketball coach of La Salle College. Gola, who was working as a Pennsylvania state representative, was La Salle's twelfth head coach in the basketball team's history. Gola wanted to bring La Salle back to the level of success he had experienced when he played at 20th and Olney.

"This puts La Salle in a difficult position, being as school starts pretty soon, and I said that the new players were in school and the season was upon us. I said what I would like to do is help out if I could," Gola told the *Collegian* in December 1968.

Gola's hiring uplifted the program and got fans buzzing about the upcoming season.

"They picked the right person in Coach Gola. He was the missing piece of the puzzle," Wlodarczyk says.

Gola hadn't even coached a game, yet people believed he would restore the basketball program's image.

"He never came across like 'I'm Tom Gola.' He never came across that way. He never came across that he did this and he did that. It was 'You're here. I'm coaching you. I'm the coach. Let's get this job done,'" says La Salle player Stan Witalec.

Gola wanted to bring success to the La Salle basketball program the same way he had in the 1950s. He wasn't promising a National Invitation Tournament (NIT) title or an NCAA championship, but he did pledge to help glue the basketball program back together. Gola also wanted his team to be successful off the basketball court. If one of his players wanted to skip a practice to study for classes, he had no problem in letting the student athlete do so. He believed that a strong student in the classroom would be a strong-minded player on the basketball court. Gola knew the challenges he faced following the scandal and La Salle's two-year probation from the NCAA.

"Our seniors are dead this year and our sophomores will lose one year and possibly another. Which means Kenny Durrett's senior year will be his first eligible year in the post season tournament," Gola told the *Collegian* in 1968.

Gola believed the penalty was too stiff at the time, especially for his upperclassmen players.

"By putting La Salle on probation, the NCAA was doing nothing more than hurting the boys," Gola said. "It's a shame to penalize our seniors and juniors. The people responsible for the infractions have been removed."

Gola laid down new rules for his players, which he expected to be obeyed without his resorting to the bullying policies of other coaches. He did not plan to bring a National Basketball Association (NBA) playing style to the college game, because he believed the two would not mix well. The players on the 1968–1969 team quickly noticed the differences between Gola's and Harding's coaching techniques.

"They were like night and day between the two of them," La Salle player Ed Holzer says.

"I think it was more a relief that the players felt when they had Gola coaching as far as comparing to the strict rules of Harding," suggests Charlie Reynolds, La Salle's basketball team manager for the 1968–1969 season.

Cannon, who was entering his senior year in 1968, questioned Gola's hiring. His last season with the Explorers would see the fourth coaching change in his four years. Cannon was highly pursued by NBA teams and was focusing on postcollege life in the pros. He worried about Gola's direction and how much time he could devote to the team in 1968 while fulfilling his political duties.

"I had real questions about what his investment was going to be. I knew his schedule was very busy," Cannon recalls. "I questioned if Tom would have that kind of interest or that kind of time."

For Joe Markmann, a senior on that 1968–1969 Explorer team, having Gola come back to La Salle was special. Having grown up in the Lawncrest section of Northeast Philadelphia, Markmann had always been cognizant of La Salle. His father, Joe Markmann Sr., had taught at La Salle College for more than thirty years and served as the chair of the Accounting Department at one point.

"I grew up being very conscious of La Salle," Joe Markmann said.

When Joe was a young kid, his father used to take him to La Salle basketball games.

"I grew up idolizing Tom Gola," Markmann says. "When Tom Gola moved on from the pros, I can remember being concerned with one thing and one thing only: how was Tom Gola doing."

Gola had always wanted to come back to help La Salle in some capacity; he was just waiting for the right moment. Gola's contract with the Explorers was a four-year deal.

"My greatest coaching challenge: teaching them good, sound, man-to-man defense where they react quickly enough to help their teammates," Gola said in the 1968–1969 La Salle media guide. Acting quickly was exactly what Gola had to do himself to begin coaching just weeks before the season's start.

Gola knew that he had a lot of talent in key players Williams, Cannon, Wlodarczyk, and Taylor, all returning from the previous season. Gola would also rely heavily on his bench, which included seniors Dunphy and Markmann.

"If the starters can't do the job consistently, we have enough bench strength to substitute frequently. The boys have been working hard, so if the defense tightens up, it should be a real good year for La Salle," Gola said.

Although Gola couldn't recruit much with the season's start just weeks away, he knew exactly the kind of player he envisioned for his team on and off the court.

"I want a boy who is interested in education. If he wants to skip a practice to study, I'll let him do that. If you have an intelligent boy, he'll make you a good player. I'm not going to take a boy with bad marks. If I do, you can remind me," Gola said.

Gola's first game as the Explorers' head coach was played on December 4, 1968, at a place he knew all too well: the Palestra. The home opener pitted the Explorers against the University of Baltimore, a team La Salle hadn't faced since 1934. The style and pace of college basketball had changed dramatically since the last time the teams had played thirty-four years earlier, as the final score of that game was a mere 55 points combined, 30–25, with the Explorers taking the win. La Salle won the opener of Gola's inaugural season as head coach by 43 points against Baltimore, 100–57. Cannon led the team with 27 points, and Durrett had 12 points. Gola's coaching style was revealed to the public as he incorporated a new weave type of offense, a system that resulted in open jump shots from the foul line.

"The seniors were on a mission. We were going to prove that we were one of the best teams in the country. We might not have been able to go to the NCAA to prove it, but we were going to show that we were the best team," says La Salle player Bob Walsh.

La Salle went on a five-game winning streak in the first month of the season, with victories against Rider, Miami, Niagara, Canisius, and Albright. The Explorers' win against Niagara was a turning point for the team that season, as Gola benched Cannon for missing the team bus ride to the airport before the game. Gola had a rule as coach: if a player was late three times, he earned a one-game suspension. Gola's decision to bench Cannon was intended not to embarrass the player but to acknowledge the breach of discipline.

"That showed a guy that was willing to lose in order to maintain the simple rules that he laid out for all of the players," says La Salle basketball player Bob Walters. "You can't underestimate the message that sends throughout the whole team. It let everyone know that if Larry is going to be penalized, then the rest of us would absolutely be penalized. It really deepened the respect that everyone had for Tom Gola."

Cannon's benching turned out to be the best thing that could have happened to the Explorers just a couple games into the season: the other team members gained confidence, realizing they could win a game even without one of their best players on the court.

Next on the schedule for the Explorers was the Quaker City Tournament at the Spectrum, a tournament the Explorers had won four years earlier.

La Salle's first game in the Quaker City Tournament was against the Penn State Nittany Lions on December 27, 1968. The game was just the second time in the schools' history that the two teams had faced each other; the previous matchup was during the 1954 season. This time, the Explorers beat Penn State, 70–55, with five players scoring in double digits, led by Durrett with 20 points.

The Explorers' second game of the tournament came against the Indiana Hoosiers, whom they beat comfortably, going over the 100-point mark,

108–88. Cannon led the team with 28 points, and Durrett, Cannon, and Williams combined for 73 points. The Explorers advanced to the championship game, a date with South Carolina and their first meeting in the schools' history. South Carolina was coming off a fifteen-win season in 1967 but had only one starter returning to the team. The game was a kind of homecoming event for two South Carolina players, John Roche and Tom Owens, who had both attended La Salle Academy, a Christian Brothers institution in upstate New York. South Carolina had only four sophomores and one junior playing most of the game under head coach Frank McGuire.

The Explorers started off the game on an 8-to-3 run, but South Carolina had the 35–27 lead at the half and never looked back. La Salle was in foul trouble the entire game, with a 21-to-8 foul differential between the two teams. In 1968, there was no shot clock or five-second rule on the court, which allowed South Carolina's Roche to hold onto the ball with no time constraints. South Carolina held the ball for long possessions by just standing on the court and passing the ball around. La Salle's assistant coach, Curt Fromal, recalls Roche's control of the game.

"We did not speed up the game. The game was slow, and he controlled it. He controlled the entire game," Fromal says. "We never got into working a transition against South Carolina."

(Fromal was a former La Salle basketball player who graduated in 1965. During his time playing ball at La Salle, he tallied 787 career points and led the 1965 Explorers to the NIT.)

La Salle lost that game against South Carolina, 62–59, the Explorers' lowest scoring game of the season. La Salle Academy alums Roche and Owens combined for 40 points.

"Nobody blamed Gola. But th[e] fact that he [Gola] stood up there and took a little bit of the heat was again an indication of his personality and directness," says La Salle basketball player Bob Walters.

It was odd for the Explorers to score such a low number of points, as the team was averaging 87.5 points heading into the championship game. That season, South Carolina posted the school's first twenty-win season, with a final record of 21–7.

"I don't think anyone thought we were going to lose to them [South Carolina]. Everyone was devastated after the game. We didn't expect to lose," remembers Witalec.

Dunphy recalls Gola's being distraught after the loss to South Carolina. He believed that he should have played his starters longer before substituting a majority of his bench into the game.

"I think Tom took that loss very hard. I remember Gola saying that he wished he had a better strategy. None of us felt that way. We all felt like we should have done more and have done better. He took it upon himself, like most leaders do—take the blame and leave the credit," Dunphy says.

After the low-scoring loss to South Carolina, the Explorers won nine straight games before their biggest game of the season, against Big 5 rival Villanova at the Palestra.

"The Palestra was just a unique experience to play in those Big 5 games. If there was a better college atmosphere, it will be hard to prove it. I know it's not the longest auditorium, but when you came out onto that Palestra floor in a Big 5 game like that, the place was just electric. You could jump a foot higher then you normally did," recalls Cannon.

The Explorers were 17–1 heading into that game, averaging 89.3 points a game; their opponents were scoring an average of 69.7 points per game. The Explorers were ranked the seventh-best program in the country by the Associated Press (AP) and ninth by United Press International (UPI). Villanova was 16–2, averaging close to 73.5 points per game and ranked seventh by UPI and eighth by the AP.

"It was a big game for a lot of reasons. We were nationally ranked, and they were nationally ranked. It was a natural rivalry," Cannon says.

The starting lineup for La Salle had Cannon, Wlodarczyk, Durrett, Taylor, and Williams facing off against Villanova's Johnny Jones, Sam Sims, Howard Porter, Frank Gillen, and Fran O'Hanlon.

"Everyone just wanted to win the Big 5. It was pretty exciting. That was a big deal—two teams in the top 10 going at each other," Szczesny remembers.

In front of a large crowd at the Palestra, La Salle took a 34–33 lead heading into halftime. In the closing minutes of the game, La Salle's Durrett was accused of dunking during a play under the basket against Villanova's Jones. Dunking was an illegal shot in 1969.

"It was definitely an illegal shot," Villanova University head coach Jack Kraft told the *Philadelphia Bulletin* after the game in 1969. "His hand was over the cylinder and his hands hit the rim when he dunked the ball. You're not supposed to be allowed to dunk the ball."

The officials let the basket stand, and Durrett completed the 3-point play. Seventeen seconds later, La Salle's Williams made a quick pass to Szczesny, who scored to extend the Explorers' lead to 9 points. The Explorers won the game, 74–67. Cannon finished the game with 11 points, 11 rebounds, and 8 assists, while Durrett finished with 20 points and 15 rebounds.

"The game they played against Villanova was probably the most anticipated Big 5 game in modern history. That was a hard game to get a ticket for," says Dick Weiss, a former basketball writer for the *Philadelphia Daily News* and New York's *Daily News*.

The Explorers finished the regular season on a fourteen-game winning streak, with wins against Big 5 opponents Penn, Temple, and St. Joe's. The Explorers scored more than 100 points four times in those fourteen games. The final game of the 1968–1969 season was at the Hollinger Field House at West Chester against the Golden Rams.

"The bus trip itself was symbolic. It was like a high school game with a bus," says Cannon. "It wasn't quite the ending we all had in mind—that's for sure."

It was unusual for West Chester to host a Big 5 opponent late in the season. Hundreds waited outside the stadium to get into the game.

"That's when the reality hit everybody," recalls Witalec. With no postseason, there would be no stakes in La Salle's final showcase, despite the team's dominance all season.

Fans attending the game wanted one of two things to happen: a successful end of the road for the Explorers or a Golden Rams upset.

"Anytime we got to play anyone in the Big 5, it was like the World Series to us. It was a big deal. It was the highlight of the season," says Vic Schuster, a junior and leading scorer for West Chester in 1968.

La Salle was taken aback by its opponents' competitiveness. With the game tied at 20, Gola called a time-out. The nationally ranked Explorers were flat.

"It was kind of a festival atmosphere. It was kind of unusual," Schuster says. "People were standing up the entire game. They wanted to see this."

The La Salle players took some pride in playing the final regular-season game, but they knew the game would have no postseason implications.

"It was anticlimactic. It was a dress rehearsal," La Salle's Michuda says. "We knew there was nothing we could do about it."

La Salle pushed forward through its players' flatness in the second half and led by as many as 15 points. With forty-one seconds left in the game and the Explorers up big, Witalec fouled West Chester's Terry Lauchnor. To make the game more memorable for his 1968 team, Gola put in every senior on the team: Cannon, Taylor, Williams, Wlodarczyk, and Markmann. The crowd was chanting "NBA" for Cannon; he was set to play professionally after college. The clock reached zero, and La Salle's season was over. The game against West Chester was a disappointing win, as the 1968 season ended with a 23–1 record. Cannon and Williams finished their careers scoring more than 1,000 points as Explorers: 1,425 and 1,230, respectfully. The 23–1 record was the greatest in La Salle history, yet the team had no chance at postseason play.

"It was pretty tough getting these kids up for tonight. All of a sudden they realized that this was the end of the road," Gola said.

The team would be relegated to watching the NCAA Tournament on TV, wondering whether they could have led La Salle to the title game given the opportunity to participate in postseason play.

"It's a shame. This is a fine basketball team and I think we could have gone quite a way either in the NCAA or NIT." Gola said. "They could be playing North Carolina in the Eastern finals."

The Explorers finished the season as the fourth-best team, according to UPI's board of coaching ratings. Despite no postseason play, Gola received five coaching honors in 1968, including College Coach of the Year Awards from the Philadelphia Sports Writers Association and the Metropolitan Basketball Writers Association.

Players on the 1968–1969 team believe that La Salle could have won the NCAA championship if the team had been allowed to participate in postseason play.

"That team we had . . . if any team could have beat UCLA [University of California, Los Angeles] . . . it was La Salle University. We could have beat them. I believe that," says Taylor. "Man for man, we were better. I think it was totally unfair what they did to us."

The UCLA Bruins, under head coach John Wooden, won the 1969 NCAA championship with star player Lew Alcindor, later known as Kareem Abdul-Jabbar.

Forward Lynn Shackelford was a senior on the 1969 UCLA national championship team. A California native who had attended John Burroughs

High School in Burbank, Shackelford says he never heard of La Salle during his team's championship run. The hype surrounding the La Salle team did not reach basketball fans in California.

"I knew very little about La Salle. I never really heard about La Salle except maybe from a newspaper or something like that," Shackelford says.

The UCLA Bruins won their first national championship in 1964 and repeated in 1965. From 1967 to 1973, UCLA would win seven straight national titles. La Salle might have had an unprecedented season in 1969, but UCLA's dynasty under Coach Wooden and the dominance of Alcindor were unstoppable.

"They might have had a pretty good basketball team at La Salle, but when it's all said and done, how in the world were they going to handle Lewis Alcindor when nobody else could?," Shackleford recalls.

During the 1968–1969 season, La Salle averaged 89 points per game (twenty-four games played), and UCLA played thirty games, averaging 84.7 points per game. La Salle finished second behind UCLA in the final AP poll at the end of the year.

"I would have liked to have [had] the opportunity to play against them [UCLA]. It was something you want to win and something you would want to do. I think that team [La Salle] was that good, I really do," Szczesny says.

"That was the best team, and that will always be the best team Philadelphia ever sees at the collegiate level," according to Cannon, who would move on to play professional ball. "It would have been fun to see what we could have done in the tournament. There is no doubt . . . that a lot of people felt like we could have challenged UCLA."

"That will always be, I guess, something that we will all regret. That we couldn't play against those types of teams and play UCLA in the final," says Walsh.

"It was hard. As I recall, it was a pretty empty feeling. We've had this speculator year—a lot of people were doubting us as one of the few teams that could beat UCLA. Could we have? We'll never know," Dunphy says.

Gola believed that if his La Salle team had not been on postseason probation, they might have met UCLA in the NCAA Tournament.

"That was the best team that La Salle ever had, including all the teams I played for," Gola said in *Palestra Pandemonium: A History of The Big 5*, by Robert Lyons. "I thought that we would have had a great shot against Lew Alcindor and UCLA. With the pressure that we could have put on defensively between Fatty Taylor and Bernie Williams, we could have contained them from getting the ball to Alcindor."

To this day, Philadelphia basketball fans believe that the 1968–1969 team is one of the best Big 5 teams of all-time.

"We always thought it was a special year, but when somebody else says it that's not part of La Salle basketball, that's when it really takes on a special meaning," Dunphy says. "There's been a lot of good teams in the city over the years, but when they put us up at the top of the class, that's pretty cool."

Gola's first season as La Salle's head coach was over, but the bitter taste of not being allowed to qualify for the postseason would remain, as the Explorers had one more year of their probation ban. It was on to another long regular season of basketball with Gola and the Explorers.

In the 1969–1970 season, Gola's second year as coach, the Explorers were in rebuilding mode. The La Salle Athletic Department lost its director, Jim Henry, following the 1968 season. Henry had had a long tenure at 20th and Olney, serving thirty-five years at the helm. John Conboy, a 1950 La Salle graduate, was hired as the new head of athletics.

La Salle lost six key players from the previous season due to graduation: Cannon, Markmann, Szczesny, Taylor, Williams, and Wlodarczyk. Cannon went on to be drafted into the NBA before later playing in the American Basketball Association (ABA) for the Miami Floridians, Taylor played in the Basketball Association of America (BAA) for the Washington Capitols, Williams played in the NBA for the San Diego Rockets, and Wlodarczyk was picked up by the NBA's Milwaukee Bucks. (Taylor passed away in December 2017 after battling breast cancer.)

"There will never be another team like that," Cannon says. "The reason for that is real simple: you'll never have that many seniors who [would go on] to become professional players."

In 1969, Jorge Garayta was a sophomore at La Salle College. He tried out for the 1969 basketball team but was one of the last guys to be cut from the official roster. A year later, Garayta laced his shoes for another tryout, but for the second straight year, he failed to make the team. In January 1970, Garayta walked into Gola's office and asked to be on the team, as the Explorers' roster was running thin due to injuries. Knowing of Garayta's past tryouts, Gola gave him a spot.

"He got the fact that I was busting my ass just to try and make the team," Garayta says. "He appreciated it."

Dunphy and Durrett were named co-captains for the 1969–1970 La Salle season. Durrett was the only returning starter from the 1968 season, and the Explorers lacked depth, height, and experience heading into Gola's second year as coach.

"Coming off last year's 23–1 performance, anything short of a spectacular season would have to be a rebuilding year, especially when you consider the boys we lost. Players like Larry Cannon and Bernie Williams won't be easy to replace. There are some bright spots, though, and the team could surprise," Gola writes in the 1969–1970 La Salle basketball media guide.

The Explorers started out the season on a two-game winning streak against Hofstra and Albright. In December, the Explorers traveled south to Knoxville, Tennessee, for the Volunteer Classic, where they defeated Yale but lost to hometown favorite Tennessee, 55–47. A week later, the Explorers played in the Quaker City Tournament at the Spectrum, beating Georgia, Cornell, and Columbia.

For the remainder of the season, La Salle lost ten of its last sixteen games, highlighted by a four-game losing streak to Creighton, Duquesne, Penn, and Canisius. The Explorers went winless against Big 5 teams in the 1969–1970 season. La Salle finished the year 14–12, the most losses in a season since the 1966–1967 season under head coach Joseph Heyer. Gola's second year as head coach was his last, as he decided to focus on politics instead of balancing his elected position with coaching La Salle basketball. Gola helmed the La Salle basketball program for only seventeen months but accomplished more than what many thought was possible in such a short period of time. At the press conference to announce his resignation, Gola stated his desire to continue to help the school from afar.

"I informed the college that I will be available as an interested alumnus to consult and advise when asked, concerning athletic matters. I also intend to maintain close contacts with the ballplayers I have had the pleasure of coaching, and I will always maintain a personal interest in La Salle and its athletic program," Gola told the *Collegian* in February 1970.

"There were occasions. Probably more than I even thought about where once or twice or a couple times a week, he [Gola] would call me sometime during the day and ask if I [could] handle practice because [he] couldn't get there. I pretty much did a lot of that," recalls Fromal.

Fromal, who was in his second year as the assistant head coach under Gola, heard the news of Gola's departure while heading home following a scouting trip to Reading, Pennsylvania. He remembers hearing the breaking news announcement over the radio.

"Tom Gola resigns from La Salle," the announcer said.

To Fromal's surprise, the announcer said that Gola was recommending that the assistant be promoted to the head coaching position. Fromal was greeted with multiple messages left on his answering machine, and his phone kept ringing throughout the night. The twenty-eight-year-old assistant coach felt confused and hurt by Gola's departure and by the fact that they had never discussed the possibility of his being promoted. The following morning, Gola and Fromal spoke on the phone about the situation. Gola offered him support with recruiting or anything he needed if he got the job.

Fromal was competing with Paul Westhead for the position. Westhead was then an assistant coach at St. Joseph's College and a 1961 graduate. Westhead ended up getting the head coaching job at La Salle, a decision that hurt Gola and Fromal.

"They hired a St. Joe guy," Fromal says.

Westhead signed a four-year contract with La Salle in 1970 but ended up staying at La Salle for nine years. His first year, he posted a 20–7 record, and his team was ranked as high as tenth in the country. In his tenure with the Explorers, they made it to the NCAA Tournament twice.

During the 1970–1971 season, Durrett tore a ligament in his knee during a game against Canisius at the Spectrum. He and the Explorers hobbled their way into the NIT that year but lost to Georgia Tech, 70–67, at Madison Square Garden.

"It was quite a difficult recovery. He was never the same after that," recalls Anna, Durrett's first wife.

Durrett's career at La Salle was historic. In seventy-one games played, he scored 1,679 points, averaging 23.7 per game. In 1971, he was selected to the All-American second team and chosen as the Big 5's Most Valuable Player (MVP). (Durrett also was MVP of the Big 5 in 1969 and 1970.)

"Kenny was such a unique player. He was a mixture of a guard and a forward who could give you a headache right away because he was so fast and he could jump so quickly. He was one of a kind," Garayta says.

Durrett was selected fourth overall in the 1971 NBA draft by the Cincinnati Royals. His contract with the Royals was reportedly worth more than $1 million. Even though Gola was not his coach anymore, he guided

Durrett through the process of dealing with agents and finances upon entering the NBA.

"He looked out for Kenny. He protected him," Anna says. "He had Kenny's back all of the way."

His professional basketball career lasted four years, playing with the Royals, the Kansas City–Omaha Kings, and the Philadelphia 76ers. Durrett passed away from a heart attack in 2003.

In April 2016, Gola's 1968–1969 La Salle team was inducted into the Big 5 Hall of Fame. Four other Big 5 teams were inducted, including the 1970–1971 Penn Quakers, the 1984–1985 Villanova Wildcats, the 1987–1988 Temple Owls, and the 2003–2004 Saint Joseph's Hawks. Years after their careers at La Salle had ended, Durrett's and Cannon's numbers were retired, with the Athletic Department hanging the "33" and "20" jerseys from the rafters.

12

....

Gola's Political Career
Begins

WILLIAM MEEHAN was a neighborhood guy from Rising Sun Avenue in Northeast Philadelphia. A graduate of La Salle College High School and the University of Notre Dame, Billy, as friends called him, was raised in the political world under his father, Austin Meehan, who was the head of the Republican Party in Philadelphia from 1961 to 1994. Later, after his father's death in the early 1990s, Billy became the general counsel for the Republicans' city committee. Billy Meehan was a political boss who understood the importance of modern technology in politics and was the glue that held the Republican Party together in the 1960s.

"Bill Green [the former mayor of Philadelphia] had a saying: My dad got a boxcar full of orange juice out of a case of oranges," Billy's son, Michael Meehan, says.

After Tom Gola retired from the NBA, Billy Meehan urged him to run for the state legislature in 1966. Gola and Meehan's friendship was nothing new, as the two had interacted when Meehan had coached him in a summer basketball league in the early 1950s.

"I often thought of being in politics," Gola told the *Philadelphia Daily News* in January 1967. "Politically, I couldn't do too much while playing basketball because of the traveling. I [was] approached years ago to run for public office, but I felt I couldn't devote the time to it before. When I retired, the reapportionment opened up in the district in which I live, so I decided to run."

Gola decided to run for local office in the 170th Legislative District, the Thirty-Fifth and Sixty-Third Wards. The 170th Legislative District included working-class neighborhoods, such as Somerton, Chalfont, Millbrook, Parkwood, and part of Bustleton. Gola structured his campaign messaging around his last name, with each letter standing for a principle. On his campaign flyer that was handed out to voters, G stood for growth, O for organization, L for leadership, and A for ability. On the back of the flyer was a letter from President Dwight D. Eisenhower asking him to attend a White House luncheon to influence the younger generation to participate more actively in sports. To add to his credibility, Gola had photos included on the flyer with John Tabor, the state secretary of commerce, and Ray Broderick, the candidate for lieutenant governor. With no political experience, Gola was hoping that his name would carry him into office.

"Gola was a part of the history of Northeast Philly when I grew up," says Jonathan Saidel, a former Philadelphia city controller. "What do you want from a politician? You want somebody who's doing what is right . . . who's gonnå stand up and do that right thing. He had a history of being a stand-up kid. A stand-up man. He knew [the difference] between right and wrong, and that's 80 percent of the game."

Gola was running against the Democrat Paul McSorley for the 170th Legislative District's seat in the state's House of Representatives. On November 9, 1966, Gola won the election with 12,780 votes to McSorley's 10,723, beating his opponent in a traditionally Democratic section of Philadelphia.

"The one thing you didn't have to worry about [with] Tom was that you didn't have to spend a fortune on name recognition, because everybody knew who he was," recalls Bill DeMarco, the manager of Gola's first campaign.

The 1967 Pennsylvania Manual for the Commonwealth of Pennsylvania Department of Public Instruction reports that a state representative received a salary of $7,200 per year and an additional $4,800 for expenses. Gola's emphasis on growth, organization, leadership, and ability did not take long to pay off. Gola worked diligently with Philadelphia and state leaders to bolster the education system and to promote labor and economic growth during his tenure as a state representative.

Gola had long valued the benefits of education, an attitude that continued throughout his life. As a state representative, Gola voted to raise the minimum salary for public school teachers to at least $5,400 (about $40,700 in 2017 dollars), or, if school funding permitted, to $6,000 ($45,300 in 2017 dollars). The legislature passed a new school funding formula benefiting the Philadelphia system, which also increased appropriations for higher education assistance to help more students attend college. He also increased the pension for retired teachers and funding for special education. In addition to working for public education, Gola helped private colleges and universities finance their building programs by creating a Higher Education Facilities authority. Gola also sponsored legislation to benefit nonpublic schools and their teachers' salaries.

Gola served on many committees as a state representative, including the Higher Education Committee, the Law and Order Committee, the Labor Relations Committee, and the Municipal Cooperation Committee. As a member of the Law and Order Committee, Gola sponsored legislation to create a state crime commission and to increase the state police force. Gola served on a task force that studied the juvenile court system in Pennsylvania, which reexamined the criteria for trying juveniles as adults. Gola additionally sponsored legislation to create a Land and Water Conservation and Reclamation Fund, providing criteria for municipalities to acquire land for recreational services and state forests.

Gola's interest in the growth of Philadelphia's economy did not mean that he neglected the working people of his district. He helped raise unemployment benefits from $45 to $60 per week. He also helped increase worker's compensation benefits for total disability from $52.50 to $60 per week and for partial disability from $42 to $45. In 1966, he increased literacy and occupational training opportunities to help people on assistance qualify for employment. In 1971, he voted to raise the state's minimum wage from $1 to $1.60 per hour, matching the federal rate.

"He was one of the few people that I can say that never or rarely . . . had . . . anything negative to say about anyone else in government or politics," says Larry Kane, a former Philadelphia television news broadcaster.

In 1968, Gola was up for reelection against the Democrat Walter Sullivan. Sullivan called for Gola to withdraw as a candidate and questioned Gola's attendance at meetings and votes in Harrisburg, the state capital. Sullivan, who was a trial lawyer, said he would not practice law on the side if elected but instead devote his full energy and attention to the fifty thousand people of the 170th Legislative District.

"Directing his energies to La Salle's high-powered basketball program and attempting to command a major voice in the Harrisburg chamber present a serious conflict [for Gola]," Sullivan told the *Philadelphia Inquirer* in August 1968.

Gola responded to the *Philadelphia Inquirer*, "If he gets all of the Democratic legislators in Philadelphia to give up their outside occupations, I'll resign."

Gola added that about 195 of the 203 state representatives were attorneys, insurance agents, farmers, and real-estate agents. Because of the low yearly salary and expenses allotment for a state representative, Gola believed that people in these positions needed to keep their side jobs. In his first two years in the legislature, Gola personally answered six hundred letters and covered the mailing costs himself.

Gola would go on to defeat Sullivan in the election, 3,639 to 2,579 votes.

"I always felt that I had a built-in public relations office with the name I got through basketball," Gola told the *Philadelphia Daily News*. "But I didn't get the name. I felt I earned it."

13

· · · · · · · ·

They're Younger, They're Tougher, and Nobody Owns Them

IN MARCH 1969, Tom Gola announced his candidacy for city controller of Philadelphia. The Republican committee unanimously endorsed
him. He was opposed by Charles "Chuck" Peruto, a forty-two-year-old
criminal attorney.

"For me, it's politics. I'm in it to stay as long as the people will have me,"
Gola told the *New York Times* in 1969.

At the same time, Arlen Specter was running for reelection as Philadelphia's nineteenth district attorney. He was opposed by the Democratic candidate David Berger and the third-party candidate Richard Ash. Specter
was coming off a losing bid in 1967 for the mayor of Philadelphia; James
Tate had won that election by fewer than eleven thousand votes. Knowing
Gola's popularity in the city, and knowing Specter's track record as district
attorney, Billy Meehan slated Gola and Specter together in 1969. They were
a perfect match. On one side, Specter would bring his political experience
and connections to the campaign; on the other, Gola would bring his brief
political experience and basketball fan voters to the polls.

"It was a very good combination ethnically. They just balanced each
other very well. My father was more white collar, and Gola was more blue
collar. It was just a great combination," says Shanin Specter, Arlen's son.

Elliott Curson, a Philadelphia advertising agency owner, and David

Garth, a New York native, were hired as political consultants for Gola's and Specter's respective campaigns. The campaigns' joint slogan was "They're younger, they're tougher, and nobody owns them."

"People loved it," says Curson.

Garth and Curson also came up with other political slogans, including "Tough young men for tough hard jobs" and "We need these guys to watch those guys." The first of these slogans won Garth a national advertising award. However, Curson wanted credit for his role in its conception. From that moment on, tension simmered between Curson and Garth regarding who came up with what slogan and who deserved the credit for the campaigns' success.

"They were a golden pair [Gola and Specter]. They ran a campaign that people still talk about today. They had slogans that were prize winners," says Shanin.

Curson put together what he considers to be his best work in any of his campaign assignments. He sent a campaign worker with a tape recorder to the corner of Broad and Chestnut Streets, hoping to get some sound bites from potential voters. Curson instructed the campaign worker to ask random Philadelphians whether they knew who the current city controller was. Many said no, which was the answer Curson was looking for. What started as an off-the-cuff experiment turned into a political innovation that put the campaigns ahead of the curve.

"I made that into a commercial," he says.

Curson and his team made a TV and radio spot from the audio content. The message behind the ads: the people of Philadelphia needed a city controller whom they knew, and that was Gola. Curson says that he ensured that every TV commercial had text at the top of the screen saying that it was paid for by the committee to elect Specter and Gola for district attorney and city controller.

"The commercial was a big hit," Curson recalls.

Gola and Specter needed to spend very little of their own money for the campaign in 1969, as the funds came directly from Meehan and the Republican Committee of Philadelphia. To formulate strategies, Curson, Garth, and their team of consultants would meet Meehan, Gola, and Specter weekly at the Bellevue Hotel in Center City. The forward thinking of Garth and Curson was a political campaigning style that Philadelphia had not seen before.

"It was really a very professional campaign of the modern type that Philadelphia hadn't seen very much of before 1969," Shanin says.

The Specter and Gola campaigns had a lot going for them in 1969. Specter was young and energetic, and since he had become the district attorney in 1965, the major crime rate around the country had risen 52 percent, while it had increased by less than 3 percent in Philadelphia, per the campaign's brochure. If Specter was reelected, he vowed, he would prosecute the repeat criminals and the gangs wandering the city. Gola believed the people of Philadelphia had the right to know exactly how and where the city's money was being spent. In his campaign, Gola said that he would speak out against favoritism, overpayments, and unnecessary contracts being handed out within the city. His plan was to restore credibility and leadership to the city controller position, and he promised loyalty to his supporters.

Peruto, Gola's Democratic opponent, was a Philadelphia native who had attended St. Joseph's University for his undergrad studies and become a criminal lawyer in the city after graduating from Temple Law School. He believed that his political experience as an assistant district attorney would help him win the city controller position.

His son, Chuck Peruto Jr., was thirteen years old when his father was running for the city controller position. Now a defense attorney, Peruto Jr. remembers campaigning door to door, attending neighborhood meetings, and going to coffee meet-ups with his father and his campaign team. He remembers a debate sometime prior to the election between Gola and his father at Bok Technical High School in South Philadelphia. The debate was a big moment for both candidates, as it was one of only two debates preceding the election.

"As a little kid, I figured my dad is running against this guy, Tom Gola. So, they must hate each other," Peruto Jr. says.

Prior to the debate, Peruto Jr. and his family went backstage, where he saw his father and Gola putting makeup on for TV. To his surprise, the two men were laughing and talking to each other. Even in a competitive situation, Gola's cheery and positive personality engaged his political challenger. It's not every day that Democrats or Republicans competing for the same position end up actually liking each other, but Gola's notoriety made Democrats cross the aisle.

"The two of them were joking around like they were best friends," Peruto Jr. recalls. "It left a mark on me because I just expected something totally different."

After five minutes of conversation between the two candidates, the debate began. Within minutes, Peruto Sr. showed a completely different side toward Gola.

"My father treated him like a skunk. Like a rotten animal. Stepped on him and just destroyed him," Peruto Jr. says. "I just couldn't believe it. How could they turn it on and off like that?"

The debate continued with various viewpoints and disagreements coming from both sides to justify their qualifications for office. At the end of the debate, Peruto Sr. challenged Gola to a foul shooting contest the day after the debate, a joke that made the audience burst into laughter. He had no basketball background, of course. Gola got a good laugh out of the joke, but the free throw contest never happened.

On the way back from the debate, Peruto discussed with his son the ins and outs of politics during that time. His father liked Gola, and sometimes not every politician hated the opponent. In fact, Peruto did not really want to be city controller.

"Neither one of them had any business being city controller," Peruto Jr. says.

His father wanted the district attorney seat and was running for controller to get his name known in the political landscape.

The office for the Gola and Specter campaigns was on the 1200 block of Chestnut Street in Center City. Vito Canuso was working on the small campaign staff when he realized that Specter and Gola made an unlikely but dominant team.

"There was no public conflict, but the personalities were entirely different," Canuso says.

Canuso remembers campaigning on a Saturday afternoon, walking around neighborhoods to shake hands with people and even stopping in local bars for votes. Everyone wanted to hang out with Gola and buy him a beer, whereas people wanted to offer Specter only a glass of water. As they campaigned side by side, their personality differences slowly fed a quiet competition.

"To a certain extent, there was even a little rivalry when you would walk in certain neighborhoods or certain areas. They would flock to Tom Gola as opposed to Specter," Canuso recalls.

One of the pamphlets being handed out to voters featured a photo of

Gola, Specter, and their wives holding hands and walking up the steps of the Philadelphia Museum of Art.

"You know why they were taken on the art museum steps? Because Specter wanted Gola to be two steps down," Canuso says.

Shanin Specter, who was eleven years old at the time of the 1969 campaign, saw the relationship between Gola and his father firsthand. His father taught Gola the ropes of politics and how to work a room. Specter knew the importance of going to every table and shaking hands with everybody in the room for votes. Gola was a sponge soaking in as much information as possible. Just like during his basketball days, Gola was learning and figuring out his own political game plan.

"I think my father looked up to Tom Gola, both literally and figuratively. My father was a huge sports fan his entire life. He marveled at Tom Gola's athletic accomplishments," Shanin says.

Gola's basketball achievements, his innovative campaign, and his ability to connect with people and make them feel cared for overshadowed his lack of political experience. On November 4, 1969, Gola defeated Peruto by seventy-one thousand votes to seal his victory as Philadelphia's newest city controller. Gola tallied 331,616 votes compared to Peruto's 260,342.

"My father got crushed in the election. Absolutely destroyed," Peruto Jr. says.

Peruto Jr. noted that his father remained upbeat following the loss and did not take it personally. During his campaign, Peruto Sr. was taking additional classes at Temple Law School, so the Democratic Party did not think he had campaigned properly. A reporter asked Peruto to what he attributed his loss in the election. He replied, "More people voted for the other guy."

In the district attorney race, Specter defeated opponents Berger and Ash, gaining 58 percent of the vote with a tally of 346,294. Berger came in second with 244,544 votes.

Gola's term as city controller began just a month and half after his election. His position would pay $31,500 annually. Newspaper headlines after Gola won read "Athlete Elected by Philadelphians." For the first time in the history of the city controller position, a Republican took office.

"It will be perhaps the biggest challenge of my life," Gola told the *Philadelphia Bulletin* in January 1969, describing his campaign. "I can promise that the tax dollars will be spent with efficiency, honesty, and fiscal responsibility."

Gola's new gig at city hall would finally put his La Salle accounting degree to good use. As the city controller, Gola was the auditor of the books and records of the city of Philadelphia and its school district. Gola's job was to investigate corruption and government irregularities in city business that used state and federal funds.

"A Democrat or Republican didn't mean anything. He just got things done. He wanted to accomplish something and worked within the system to try to get things done, whether the votes were Democrat or Republican," says Martin Weinberg, a former city solicitor in Philadelphia.

Gola's ability to work effectively with the Democratic and Republican leaders of Philadelphia would help his 1973 campaign, when he and Specter were up for reelection.

14

....

1973 City Controller
Reelection

IN NOVEMBER 1973, Tom Gola and Arlen Specter once again campaigned together in their bids for reelection. Gola was up against William Klenk, a Democrat and former assistant city solicitor, and Specter was running against Emmett Fitzpatrick, a former Philadelphia assistant district attorney.

Before Gola took office, no one knew who the city controller was or what someone in that position did for the city. After four years in the position, Gola was confident that Philadelphia's tax dollars were being spent wisely. Gola and his team conducted twice as many city audits as had the previous city controller, Alexander Hemphill. Hemphill had served as the city controller from 1957 to 1968 before resigning to make a primary run for the mayor of Philadelphia, but the West Chester native had lost in the mayoral primary against James Tate.

Gola had revamped the city's investment policies, which expanded Philadelphia's revenue by almost $1 million. If reelected, Gola pledged to continue helping the city of Philadelphia not waste money under his watch.

As the city's district attorney from 1966 to 1974, Specter had prosecuted criminals, uncovered corruption, and ensured that due process was being served. He wanted to see higher conviction rates in murder and rape cases, and to this end, he pledged to increase staffing within the Philadelphia Police Department.

For the campaign, Specter's and Gola's political teams created a pamphlet with bold red Helvetica text against a black background featuring information on both candidates. Big red and white letters on the front read "People like Specter and Gola." The handout contained key information on various topics, such as reforming the political system, cutting corruption, and protecting Philadelphians' legal rights. It included photos of the two men shaking hands with business leaders and families around the city. The pamphlet read, "Specter and Gola. You know you can trust them. Doesn't it make sense to keep them?" and "This year, it's good to find people in government fighting crime and corruption."

The candidates' headquarters, run by the "Citizens for Specter and Gola Campaign Committee," was located in the 200 American Patriot Building on 112 South 16th Street in Center City. Reelection was looking like a lock for Specter and Gola, and so the two took a step back from heavy campaigning, thinking they had the election in the bag.

"Everybody expected Specter and Gola to get reelected. There was no question in anybody's mind," says Frank Buzydlowski, a polling volunteer for the Gola and Specter campaigns.

Even Gola's long-time friend John Chaney, who would later coach for Temple University, planned to vote for Gola and the Republican Party.

"He was the only Republican I would vote for. Not any Republican assholes. Not at all," Chaney says. "He was always someone who was generous. He had a great deal of humility. And he had a personality that you could look deep into his soul and see that he was a good soul person. He was just misguided because he was a Republican."

On June 17, 1972, the now-infamous Watergate break-in took place at the Democratic National Committee headquarters in Washington, D.C., where members of the Republican Party, under the direction of President Richard Nixon, stole top-secret documents and bugged office phones. The controversy, which led to Nixon's resignation in 1974, sent shockwaves throughout the country, primarily affecting the Republican Party. Its future was uncertain. Voters did not know who to trust in upcoming elections.

"I said to the guys, 'You better be careful. I'm out on the street, I'm out shopping, and nobody knows you are running,'" Caroline Gola recalls telling her husband.

Gola's opponent, William Klenk, a Chestnut Hill resident, stated in his campaign that Gola was not doing his job as city controller. If elected, Klenk would push for regional financing. Gola and Klenk traded jabs throughout their campaigns, as Klenk believed that Gola did not use quality control, program auditing, and priority accounting during his time in office.

Gola had increased the Philadelphia budget to $180,000 over the three and a half years of his tenure. He also had created twenty-two new positions, which increased the number of audits from 57 in 1971 to 105 in 1972.

"We've upgraded the office by bringing back professionalism. Work in our office is now recognized as a credit toward the CPA, which it never was in the past," Gola said in a debate against Klenk.

Just days prior to the 1974 election, the *Philadelphia Daily News* endorsed Gola for reelection. The newspaper noted its disappointment in Klenk's criticism of Gola's past performance as controller, stating that it was abstruse and vague. Just forty-eight hours later, the *Philadelphia Inquirer* endorsed Gola as well. However, the *Inquirer* did not endorse Specter because it was no secret that he planned to eventually run for governor of Pennsylvania.

On election night, Gola and Specter were headquartered in the Constitution Room of the Sheraton Hotel in Center City, and the Democrats held their reception in the Burgundy Room of the Bellevue-Stratford Hotel. Even with the support of the Philadelphia papers, election night did not go as planned for Gola and Specter: Gola lost to Klenk by fewer than seven thousand votes, 212,416 to 205,615. Specter lost reelection for the district attorney position to Fitzpatrick by thirty thousand votes.

"Republicans just didn't show up at the polls. It wasn't people voting Democrat out of protest. The Republicans just stayed home that year. It was a complete shock," says Alan Butkovitz, the Philadelphia city controller from 2006 to 2017.

Paul Giordano, a supporter of the Gola and Specter campaigns in 1974, attended the election night party in Center City. He recalls that the mood in the room quickly went from a party atmosphere to funereal after the announcement was made that the Gola and Specter bids had been defeated. On the inside, Gola was distraught, but he displayed a sense of confidence and encouragement to his supporters.

"*He* lost the election, and he was worried about *me*. He was worried about me because he saw me going crazy crying. It was just the saddest night of all of our lives. But he was so strong. He was holding us up," Giordano says.

Gola's run as city controller was over, and so was Specter's tenure as district attorney. The younger and tougher all-star team had been blind-sided by Klenk and Fitzpatrick.

"It was shocking. Totally shocking," says Canuso, a member of Gola's and Specter's campaign staff in 1974. He speculates that national politics may have hurt Republican chances in local elections: "Watergate killed Specter and Gola."

Gola's and Specter's losses were influenced by the low voter turnout. In 1974, there was a 43 percent voter turnout, which was 180,000 fewer votes than had been cast in the past three elections. Just over a million people registered to vote in the 1974 election, but only 432,847 actually voted. Private polls prior to the election predicted that Specter would get 60 to 75 percent of the vote, but the polls failed to indicate how many of those polled would actually end up voting on Election Day.

"If the percentage of the turnout had been anywhere close to where it was in 1969, Specter and Gola would have been reelected," Canuso believes.

The Specter and Gola teams had largely stayed home on election night, believing that they were going to win their respective positions. Republican leaders had been sure that the 1974 election would yield a high turnout.

"Gola and my father, I think, were both very surprised to be defeated," Shanin says.

At the Democratic headquarters on election night, then-governor Milton Shapp and Democratic chairman Peter Camiel proclaimed that democracy was returning to Philadelphia.

"Had it not been for Watergate, Tom Gola would have wound up being mayor of Philadelphia. He would have easily been reelected as city controller," says Buzydlowski.

After losing the district attorney election, Specter ran for Pennsylvania's U.S. Senate seat in 1976 but lost to fellow Republican H. John Heinz III.

"The loss of that [1974] election created a monster out of Specter. He was determined to get back into the national or statewide politics," says Larry Kane, a Philadelphia broadcasting legend.

In 1978, Specter lost in the primary for governor of Pennsylvania to Dick Thornburgh. Specter would later become a U.S. Senator in 1981. He passed away from complications due to non-Hodgkin's lymphoma at age eighty-two in 2012.

A day after Gola's defeat in the 1974 election, then-mayor Frank Rizzo wrote him a letter expressing his thoughts on the loss.

"But even in defeat, we manage sometimes to come up with an even better outlook. In your case, with your great talent and your youth, there are no horizons that you can't reach, and if I can help in any way, you can depend on me," Rizzo wrote.

Harvey Schley, a campaign worker for the Gola and Specter campaigns in 1974, said that Rizzo had frequently visited Gola's city controller office.

"Everybody liked Tom Gola. Frank Rizzo, who was a Democrat, even liked Tom Gola," Schley says.

Prior to the election, Gola and Caroline had made plans to vacation in Maine regardless of the outcome. But even in defeat, Gola decided that he would ditch the vacation plans and stay at work to finish out the year.

"How many freaking guys do you know that lose their job and they are going to get paid anyway and they are saying they can't take a vacation because 'I have a job to do'?" asks Mo Gola.

Gola's political career was over for the time being, but he would place his name on another ballot in 1983.

15

....

Tom Gola for Mayor

IN NOVEMBER 1982, then-mayor of Philadelphia William Joseph Green announced that he would not seek reelection. Candidates began to line up for the chance to take his office on behalf of the Democratic and Republican Parties, with Democrats Thomas Leonard, the current city controller, and Wilson Goode, the city's managing director, emerging as contenders for the head post at city hall.

Just after Christmas 1982, Billy Meehan, the Republican Party leader, and John Egan, the chair of the Philadelphia Stock Exchange, discussed the possibility of Egan's changing parties to run on the Republican ticket for the May 17 primary. He agreed, even though he was heavily involved with the Democratic Party.

Even though Gola had been away from politics since 1974, he gradually regained interest in running for political office again, getting the itch to start a campaign to become the next mayor of Philadelphia. Gola was disappointed that Meehan, his long-time friend, endorsed another candidate for mayor. For the first time in Gola's political career, the then-fifty-year-old candidate was anxious, feeling his back against the wall while he pursued a position he wanted.

"By the time he decided he was going to do it [run for mayor], my father

[had] already committed himself to John Egan," says Mike Meehan, Billy's son. "When he [Billy] gave you his word, he would not change."

Meehan kept his word, and the Republican Party supported and endorsed Egan's spot in the upcoming primary. Gola had been grooming himself for a mayoral run for a couple of years, but he had never told anyone. Gola said he had told Meehan in December 1982 that he wanted to run for mayor, but the GOP leader did not know whether he intended to actually follow through.

Gola decided his ambitions for the mayor's office were not over, despite not having Meehan's support, and he formed a campaign committee to officially run on the Republican mayoral ticket. On January 23, 1983, Gola announced his campaign at the Philadelphia Centre Hotel and hired Philadelphian Lorenzo Gay to be his campaign manager and the heavyweight political consultant Roger Stone as an adviser. Stone had organized Ronald Reagan's campaign for president in the Northeast in 1980 and Thomas Kean's successful run for governor of New Jersey in 1981.

"I'm anxious to compare my Republican credentials with John Egan's in these open forums," Gola said in a press release in February 1983. "I just don't believe city Republicans want to nominate a Democrat as their candidate."

"I'm pleased with the broad cross-section of businessmen, entrepreneurs, and community leaders who have joined our effort," Gola continued. "I'm confident they can raise the resources necessary for victory."

Gola charged his finance committee with raising the $500,000 he had budgeted for his primary campaign. Gola named Warren "Pete" Musser, the chair of the board of Safeguard Scientifics, as the chair of this finance committee; Robert Butera, the president of the Philadelphia Flyers, was appointed co-chair of Gola's campaign committee.

"A lot of people ask me why would I want to be mayor, why do I need the headaches," Gola said to the *Philadelphia Daily News* during his campaign run. "But they always do it from a pessimistic point of view, where they feel Philadelphia can't be turned around. I disagree."

To officially launch his campaign, Gola had to resign from his regional administrator position with the U.S. Department of Housing and Urban Development (HUD). Gola thought he had a "good shot" at the mayor's seat, even though Democrats outnumbered Republicans in Philadelphia at the time by more than a three-to-one ratio. The Republican mayoral primary was set, with Egan, Gola, and the former U.S. representative Charles Dougherty vying for the nomination. Gola believed that Meehan's refusal to endorse him was unfair and that the endorsement of a Democrat for the Republican nomination was a threat to the continued health of the Republican Party in the city.

"Billy made a mistake, and you talk about loyalty—no one can question my loyalty to the Republican party," Gola said to the *Philadelphia Daily News* in 1983. "I'm running for the survival of the Republican party."

Gola and his team planned on raising $500,000 for the primary campaign that May, with that money earmarked for a heavy focus on television and radio advertising.

"Look, I could move out to Montgomery County tomorrow and be in the majority party. But I won't do that," Gola said to the *Philadelphia Daily News* in 1983. "I was born and raised in Philadelphia. I've lived here all my life. And I think things can be done in this city. I really do."

His other campaign team members were Constance Wolf, Musser, Butera, Chris Gigliotti Jr., Paul Jaffe, Dick Ireland, and Anthony "Skip" Minisi, who already were forming a finance committee for when the funds came in. Gola was receiving pledges from supporters but faced financial difficulties since he wasn't backed by the Republican Party of Philadelphia.

"I just feel it's the right time to put all of my experience together and do something for the city. If the people say no, that's fine, I'm not dependent on politics for a living," Gola said.

Gola believed he was the strongest candidate for the Republican primary ticket. His plan was to focus on economic growth that would bring jobs to the city and crack down on crimes that threatened the safety of Philly neighborhoods.

"I will bring to the mayor's office my years of successful business experience. Only hard-headed business practices can bring the tough, cost-effective city management Philadelphia needs so desperately," Gola said in a 1983 letter to his supporters.

Gola's campaign was off and running with the slogan "Nobody's man but yours." His headquarters was located in the 1700 block of Market Street. Gola's peers believed that he had a chance of winning the primary if he put together a well-orchestrated campaign and capitalized on his previous political connections within the city.

"I'm more qualified," Gola said to the *Philadelphia Daily News* when asked about his opponents. "John Egan's been absolutely nowhere. Charlie Dougherty's been a school teacher and a legislator."

Egan was a high school dropout from Kensington who had become a millionaire by trading options at the Philadelphia Stock Exchange. When running for the mayoral ticket, Egan had to leave his position with the stock exchange.

Gola also believed that he had a chance to win a race against Wilson Goode, the Democratic nominee.

"I had a good rapport with the black community," Gola says in *Wilt, 1962*, by Gary Pomerantz. "I figured that, plus being city controller citywide, I thought it would work."

In February 1983, the *Philadelphia Daily News* reported that U.S. Senator Spector held a meeting with the Republican primary candidates to talk two of the three candidates out of running. Egan and Dougherty attended the meeting in Center City, but Gola did not.

"I am in the race until November," Gola said. "I will not get out. I will not make any deal."

In the meeting, Spector advised the candidates to concentrate their campaigns on personality rather than issues to enhance their appeal to a left-leaning electorate. None of the candidates followed this advice.

Egan won the Republican primary on May 17, 1983, with 45 percent of the vote, winning a total of 38,920. Dougherty came in second with 25,413 votes, and Gola came in third with 21,581 votes, or roughly 25 percent.

Some speculated that it would have been interesting to see how Gola would have fared in a two-candidate primary race.

"The way the numbers fell with Dougherty being outside of his congressional district, he was really not known by anyone. Tommy was universally known, and Dougherty being in the race probably hurt Tommy," suggests Mike Meehan.

On the night of the primary, Gola waited until 11:00 P.M. for the final votes to come in before acknowledging his supporters at the Philadelphia Centre Hotel. He sent his congratulations to Egan, Dougherty, and GOP leader Meehan.

"I feel that we got started a little late," Gola said in front of his supporters. "We may have needed a little more time. Unfortunately, it wasn't there."

On the Democratic primary side, Goode defeated Rizzo, Frank Lomento, Stephen Douglas, Anthony Bateman, and George Britt Jr. The primary was effectively a two-horse race between Goode and Rizzo, with Goode winning the election by more than fifty-nine thousand votes, or 52 percent.

"I think by '83, the Republican Party had lost the ability to take the mayor's race," says Jonathan Saidel, the Philadelphia city controller from 1990 to 2006.

In the general election in November 1983, Goode defeated Egan to become the first African American to be elected as the mayor of Philadelphia.

Gola's political career in the city had officially reached its final chapter.

16

....

One Call to Superman

THE 1985–1986 SEASON was mediocre for La Salle University. The team, led by head coach Dave "Lefty" Ervin, posted a 14–14 record but failed to make the postseason for the second year in a row. Ervin reportedly felt the pressure from the La Salle community regarding his lack of success and resigned before he could be fired following the season. The departure was a mutual breakup, as the media reported that Ervin was battling an alcohol addiction. Ervin had compiled a 119–87 record over seven seasons at the helm. La Salle officials knew that the program needed to head in a different direction—which was pointing straight to South Philadelphia.

Just miles from La Salle's campus, a young player named Lionel Simmons was turning heads with his quick ability to score baskets. Letters upon letters came pouring into the mailbox of his South Philadelphia home. Simmons had all the makings of a high-level recruit but made it known that he wanted to stay in his hometown of Philadelphia to further his education and play basketball. The only two schools he considered outside Philadelphia were Boston College and Old Dominion. Villanova and Temple were a bit late to get in on the recruiting process, so they were out of his favor. Simmons's decision came down to Saint Joseph's and La Salle.

La Salle officials understood just how important it was to land a player like Simmons. They knew they could not lose a recruit of this caliber, especially in their own backyard. But to get him, they had to get plenty of other ducks in a row first.

Simmons's recruitment started with Bill Bradshaw. Bradshaw had graduated from Bishop Duffy High School, now known as Niagara Catholic, outside Niagara Falls, New York. In December 1962, Bradshaw's high school basketball coach had asked him whether anyone on the team would be interested in being a manager for the Niagara University versus La Salle game. Bradshaw and one of his teammates had volunteered—not knowing anything about La Salle at the time—just to get a little closer to the action. He had later met La Salle star Bill Raftery at the team's hotel and become hooked on the idea of being an Explorer.

Bradshaw had attended La Salle in 1965 as a walk-on for the baseball team, playing alongside multisport athletes Fran Dunphy and Joe Markmann. The second baseman's walk-on status had lasted a year before he received a baseball scholarship and started the last three years, being named captain during his senior year. Upon graduation from La Salle in 1969, Bradshaw had been drafted by the Texas Rangers and played two years within the minor league system of the Washington Senators before breaking his ankle twice in a span of two years. After his baseball career had ended, Bradshaw had moved into the sales business.

Bradshaw had moved back to New Jersey for a job when he received a call from Gene McDonnell, his old baseball coach at La Salle College. McDonnell disclosed to Bradshaw that La Salle was looking for a new athletic director. Bradshaw knew right away that he needed that job.

"I wanted it so badly," Bradshaw said. "It was my alma mater. I studied for it. I came in, and I was ready."

Bradshaw met with Don DiJulia, Saint Joseph's long-time athletic director, before he met with La Salle's board of directors. He wanted to prepare and to have an inside track on what committees like La Salle's were looking for.

"All you have to be as athletic director is be able to walk on water and please everybody all of the time. That's what I say typically," DiJulia said.

Bradshaw participated in an interview with fifteen to twenty board members and got the job, becoming La Salle's athletic director. He was the first piece of the Simmons recruiting puzzle.

The next step was to find a head coach, preferably one who could establish a rapport with Simmons or who had a strong reputation in Philadelphia basketball. Despite much pushback, Bradshaw advocated for William "Speedy" Morris, who was currently coaching La Salle's women's basketball team. Morris was familiar with the Explorers' basketball program and where it had been. He was especially familiar with Tom Gola and his legacy at 20th and Olney.

Morris's admiration for Gola had started in 1956, when Morris was an eighth grader at St. John the Baptist in Manayunk, in the northwestern section of Philadelphia. As a member of his Catholic Youth Organization (CYO) basketball team, Morris, his teammates, and his head coaches had taken a trip down 3400 Civic Center Boulevard to Convention Hall to see Gola and the Philadelphia Warriors take on the Fort Wayne Pistons.

"I was a big-time Tom Gola guy," Morris says.

He doesn't recollect exactly how it happened, but at some point in the game, young Morris had touched Gola's hand as he ran onto the court. For a thirteen-year-old basketball fan, making contact with one of his idols was life-changing and uplifting. A kid who had listened to the radio broadcasts of the 1954 and 1955 National Collegiate Athletic Association (NCAA) Tournament championship games had gotten a brief chance to be close to his idol on the court.

"He became a hero that day," Morris says.

After St. John the Baptist, Morris had attended Roman Catholic High School, where his love for basketball only increased. In 1967, he had become the head basketball coach at his alma mater, where he had remained until 1981; he had also run various area basketball camps in the late 1960s. He had moved on to Penn Charter to coach, until one day when he got a call asking whether he had any interest in coaching the women's team at La Salle. Morris had no interest in coaching women, nor could he remember the last time he had watched any women's basketball games, even dating back to his CYO playing days. But he had agreed to meet with the Athletic Department, and La Salle had sweetened the pot by offering tuition remission for his children. That had been the deal clincher for Morris and his family; he had been named the new women's coach in 1984.

During Morris's two seasons as head coach of the women's team, his practices had sometimes featured brief appearances from Gola. Morris might spot Gola sitting in the stands of Hayman Hall, usually sporting his sweat suit from playing a pickup game on one of the other courts. Gola didn't approach Morris after practice, instead quietly walking out.

Morris's name came up in conversations about who should succeed Ervin as the coach of La Salle's men's team—but not in a positive way. Nobody on the alumni board wanted Morris as a coach, citing his lack of a college degree as the main point against him.

"I think there were some members of the faculty who maybe had some reservations concerning the fact that he didn't have a college degree. I don't think that was a major factor at that time," says Peter Filicetti, a former clinical psychology professor at La Salle for thirty-six years and the head of the athletic board.

Yet Morris had a rapport with Simmons's high school coach. In fact, Morris would bring him a pack of smokes when they met up during their days of high school coaching. Bradshaw saw this connection and knew that Morris might be the only coach who could bring Simmons to La Salle.

"There was opposition at that time by some committee members who thought we should have a more extensive search rather than simply moving Speedy from [the] women's position into the men's position," says Filicetti.

Bradshaw thought that the more time they spent debating whether Morris was qualified for the position, the smaller the chance that they could land him.

"He had an astute basketball mind. He could coach the game at any level," Bradshaw says.

The committee continued to balk at the idea of moving Morris, although Bradshaw knew in his heart that he was the perfect man for the job. Other conversations considered such candidates as La Salle alum and former Drexel coach Eddie Burke, but nothing was made official. Bradshaw knew that he was running out of time.

Bradshaw called the only person he knew who could move mountains: Tom Gola.

"I had one call . . . and it was to Superman," Bradshaw says. "I told Gola I was just afraid that the more we wait[ed], the less we [had] a chance to get him."

Gola asked what he could do to help. Bradshaw asked whether it would be possible for him to call Brother Patrick Ellis, the president of La Salle University. It couldn't hurt to have the president on your side, Bradshaw thought. Gola agreed and set up a face-to-face meeting with Brother Pat.

"There is no doubt in my mind that meeting [that] Tom Gola had with Brother Patrick put us over the hump with Speedy," Bradshaw says.

On March 7, 1985, the La Salle women were gearing up for the Metro Atlantic Athletic Conference (MAAC) championship game against St. Peter's. If they won the game, they would clinch a spot in the NCAA Tournament. Prior to shoot around, a team manager for the Explorers told Morris that he had a phone call; Morris told the manager to take a message. The caller, Bradshaw, would not wait. Morris was confused as to what Bradshaw wanted but thought perhaps it would be a good-luck chat.

Instead, Bradshaw told Morris that Ervin was out as the men's coach, and La Salle needed a new one. He asked Morris whether he wanted the job. Morris thought he would have to apply and interview for the position, but Bradshaw offered him the job on the spot, with the condition that he could not tell anybody.

"I was coaching the championship game, knowing I was going to be the new men's coach," Morris says. "I knew I was going to be the new men's coach before the game started."

Regardless, Morris's Explorers won the MAAC Tournament and clinched their first NCAA berth since 1983 under head coach Kevin Gallagher. The victory was a little bittersweet for Morris, watching his women's team celebrate after the win and knowing that he would be leaving after the next loss. La Salle lost to Villanova in the first round of the NCAA Tournament, and Morris's focus shifted to the men's team.

The second piece in the Simmons recruitment puzzle was in place. Now it was time to reel in the big fish.

As the new head coach, Morris made it his top mission to land Simmons. No matter what it would take, Simmons would be an Explorer the next season if Morris had anything to say about it.

"That was our number-one priority," he says.

One of the final recruiting meetings took place at South Philadelphia High School with Simmons and his mother, Ruth; Mitch Snyder, the head basketball coach of South Philadelphia High School; and two of Morris's bench coaches, including Dunphy.

Morris had the same pitch for many of his recruits: playing time was earned, not given, and nobody was guaranteed a spot on the team. One of Morris's assistant coaches kicked him under the table during the meeting with Simmons, because everyone knew this caveat would not be true at all.

Simmons was more talented than anyone La Salle had on the team at the time, and Morris's assistants thought the chances of landing Simmons would diminish if they told him that his playing time wasn't assured. Morris had one more thing to say to Simmons, the same thing Gola would soon tell him: "If you want to make a name for yourself in Philadelphia, you should go to a Big 5 school."

The decision of where to attend school was now entirely in Simmons's hands, yet one more person wanted to pitch the Explorer experience to him. Gola called Simmons to set up a meeting with the teenager to try to gauge his feelings. Simmons did not know much about Gola or who he was, other than his name and that he had played basketball.

Gola, Simmons, and Eddie Altieri, met at a restaurant in South Philly. Simmons was very nervous during the meeting; Altieri noted that he kept ordering Coca-Cola refills.

"I was still undecided, trying to decide between the local schools, and talking to Tom assured me that La Salle was the good choice," Simmons says.

At the dinner, Gola discussed how beneficial it would be for Simmons to go to La Salle. The two talked about the history of the program and the legacy of Philadelphia Big 5 basketball. Gola reiterated to Simmons that he would have a chance to build on his Philadelphia legacy that he had started in high school. Gola believed that Simmons would choose La Salle and have a big influence on the Philadelphia basketball community, similar to what Gola himself did in the 1950s.

"One of the main things he told me [about] was being popular and famous in your hometown. Staying home and doing well there carries a lot more weight [than] if you go out of town," Simmons says. "He made me a lot more comfortable making my decision."

That decision was to attend La Salle and play for Morris. The puzzle was complete.

Morris knew when he got Simmons that his newly minted team would be able to play with the best at the highest levels right away.

His Explorer team did just that in the 1987–1988 season, with Simmons leading the charge. He averaged 20.3 points and 9.8 rebounds per game as a freshman. The team went 20–13 for the season and made a strong charge in the National Invitation Tournament (NIT), eventually bowing out to Southern Mississippi in the finals at Madison Square Garden.

The following season, Simmons was joined by the 1987 Public League Markward award winner, Doug Overton. The Dobbins Tech student had received offers from all over the country and even considered joining former teammates Eric "Hank" Gathers and Gregory "Bo" Kimble at the University of Southern California. Before Overton could make the decision to head west, Gathers and Kimble transferred to Loyola Marymount, and Overton decided to stay in Philly.

"I said I would rather pass the ball to Lionel twenty times than to pass the ball to Hank and Bo forty times," Overton laughs.

Overton chose La Salle. He knew it was going to be a special season, knowing how well Lionel had performed in his freshman year and how Overton had been player of the year in 1987.

"I knew I was going to be playing with some great players, and then my senior year of high school, they [La Salle] made it to the NIT finals. So, obviously, I knew that it was going to be a special group, and it helped me make my decision to go there. It was exciting. I knew the legend of Speedy. I knew how great he was. He was a Philly legend," he says.

Overton was off and running with Simmons, making waves in the NCAA during the 1987–1988 season. Finishing undefeated in the Metro Atlantic Athletic Conference (MAAC), La Salle won twenty-four games and was good enough to be a thirteenth seed in the NCAA Tournament before losing to Kansas State in South Bend, Indiana. Overton's first year at La Salle was over, but he always believed that playing basketball in Philadelphia was meant to be. Playing alongside "L-Train" Simmons was an experience in itself.

"When you get there and play with somebody that good and that smart, it raises your level. It made me a better player. It made me focus more, concentrate more, think more, because he was such a high-level player. You wanted to raise your level and game to his. I think he made me better," Overton says.

The 1988–1989 season was when La Salle's basketball program really ramped up, with Simmons leading the way. The Explorers won twenty-six games that year, tying the record set back in 1955 when La Salle went 26–5 under Coach Ken Loeffler and Gola. Morris's team in 1989 made it to the NCAA for the first time since 1983, as an eighth seed. The Explorers, an eighth seed in the tournament, lost to Louisiana Tech.

Over the years, Gola would make appearances at practices and events to show his support for the program and its current players. Overton respected Gola's presence and said it didn't go unnoticed.

"I knew Lionel had a really good relationship with him. He was an important adviser for Lionel," Overton says. "It was awesome. That's what it is all about. Especially those two great players, and to see them get together like that, what he did with Lionel. I knew how much Lionel trusted him and relied on him. That's just awesome. You don't see that every day in sports."

Simmons's senior year was the 1989–1990 season, and the accolades were racking up. Morris and the Explorers went for a program-high season of 30–2, a record that still stands at 20th and Olney. La Salle went undefeated in the MAAC (16–0) and placed as a fourth seed in the NCAA Tournament, winning the first round against Southern Mississippi but losing to fifth-seeded Clemson in the second round, 79–75.

The 1989–1990 season was Simmons's last at La Salle. Simmons won the 1990 John R. Wooden Award and the Eastman Award (given by the National Association of Basketball Coaches) and was named the 1990 Player of the Year by the Associated Press (AP). To this day, he ranks third in NCAA history for scoring, behind Pete Maravich (Louisiana State University) and Freeman Williams (Portland State). For his 1987–1990 run, Simmons still holds the NCAA record for most consecutive games scoring in double figures, at 115. He is tied for third all-time in double-doubles with Derrick Coleman (Syracuse) and behind Tim Duncan (Wake Forest) and Ralph Sampson (Virginia).

Through all the trials and tribulations of picking La Salle; winning and losing a few NCAA Tournament games; and losing a dear friend in Gathers, who died at the age of twenty-three on March 4, 1990, after collapsing during a West Coast Conference tournament game, Simmons always had Gola's support when he needed it.

After graduating, Simmons needed a sports agent. He planned to enter the National Basketball Association (NBA) draft at the end of June 1990. Gola helped him select an agent and a money manager, letting him know that the agent worked for him and that Simmons could hire anyone he wanted. Simmons did not go through the normal agencies to find the right fit, as Gola helped ease that task.

"It was kind of a turning point, where I didn't go through the normal agencies of paying those guys money. He made me look into the business side of selecting an agent," he says.

Simmons listened to the Hall of Famer. He was selected seventh overall by the Sacramento Kings in the 1990 NBA draft, a draft class featuring Derrick Coleman, Gary Payton, and even his local friend Bo Kimble. Scouts and writers described Simmons as an "all-around" player, the same mantra people had applied to Gola when he played in the league. Simmons moved out west to join the Kings, and his pro career was off and running. During this period, Gola's teaching and mentoring was exactly what Simmons needed.

"Everything besides basketball, he was the guy I turned to," he says. "Not only on the court but off the court, he was an influence."

As contracts and the logistics of his new deal were flowing in, Simmons wanted to give back to his family, and he decided to look into purchasing a home for his mother, Ruth. With no prior experience in buying a home, Simmons contacted Gola for guidance. Gola helped pick out the right house and area for Ruth, as Simmons had no insight into where to look for a home. Gola showed Ruth how to handle the builders and walked her through the entire process. Gola helped Simmons with a lot of first experiences as he transitioned into a new luxurious life in the NBA. Gola's post-college guidance was exactly what Simmons needed.

"There was a lot of information that I wasn't aware of. I was greatly appreciative of getting it from him," he says.

Simmons wanted to treat himself during his first year in the league, so he purchased a 1991 Mercedes 560 SEC with, of course, Gola's help. The car was the first of its kind in 1991, and Simmons never saw the car until he came home that summer.

"Anything that was important, that was a first for me, that I needed some expertise in or I needed some guide or kind of guidance, he was always there. He was always the guy to walk me through the doors [of] bank loans and businesses," Simmons says.

17

········

The Legacy of
Number 15

THROUGHOUT HIS CAREER, Tom Gola made a significant impression on his teammates and his opponents on the court and in the political arena. It is remarkable to review the statements of those who worked with him and see the same characteristics recur: his integrity, his humility, his loyalty, and his care for others.

These characteristics were not apparent only in Gola's interactions with the powerful and the prominent. He maintained the same commitment to excellence and to helping the people around him when he was off the court and away from the spotlight. Even when no one was watching, when Gola had an opportunity to make a positive impact on the lives of the people he met, he took it. If Brother Joe Grabenstein was right, and history really does stand on the legacy of others, Gola made sure that his legacy provided a good foundation for as many histories as possible.

Gola had a busy basketball schedule when he played for the Philadelphia Warriors in the late 1950s. He adjusted to the professional lifestyle of attending practices, driving to games, and finding downtime to spend with his wife and son. Spectators loved Gola on the court, and he soon realized that he had an impact on the younger generation in Philadelphia. When Gola had an opportunity to give back to the community, he did so in a big way.

. . . .

IN 1954, a young Philadelphia native named William "Sonny" Hill attended a matchup of La Salle versus Dayton at Convention Hall. Hill traveled from his home at 16th and Dauphin Streets in North Philadelphia to the stadium. The Explorers played ten games at Convention Hall during the 1954 season. This game would be the first time Hill saw Gola and the Explorers play. He sat in the upper tier of the stadium, with his eyes glued on number 15.

"That was the first time I cast my eyes on Tom Gola," Hill says. "Tom Gola did everything but clean the basketball floor after the game."

La Salle won the game against Dayton, 82–58. Gola's presence on the court, offensively and defensively, made Hill a fan. Hill looked up to Gola.

"From that point on, I became a big Tom Gola fan," he says.

Hill graduated from Northeast Catholic High School in Philadelphia in 1955. He then attended Central State University (Ohio) for two years before playing in the semipro Eastern Basketball League for several seasons. Hill created the Sonny Hill Community Basketball League in 1968, a foundation teaching basketball and life skills to young players in the Philadelphia area. Over the years, Gola supported the league by attending a multitude of games and seeing the best young players in the city. Hill and Gola were on the same page: they wanted to give back to the community in a big way through the game of basketball.

"Both of us were [at] the same place in terms of how can we help, in terms of making the society that we live in a better place for everybody. That was the bond that we were able to form. Basketball was a way to make the connection. The bond was because of the philosophy and concept," Hill says.

Hill received the Mannie Jackson — Basketball's Human Spirit Award from the Naismith Memorial Basketball Hall of Fame in 2008.

. . . .

EVERY WEEK, the Conlogue family would drive around the Philadelphia area to look for a new place to live. Sundays had become boring to then-nine-year-old John Conlogue, as he remembered getting in his parents' car four times a month to look at potential new homes. After weeks of looking for a new place to live, the Conlogue family finally put a deposit down on a house in the Somerton section of Philadelphia, on Rennard Street, an open-country section of the city in the late 1950s. The Conlogues were satisfied with their new living arrangement and were ready for a fresh start away from their old home at Cottman and Large Street in the Rhawnhurst section of Philadelphia. A new neighborhood meant new friends, sports clubs, schools, and, of course, new neighbors.

"I didn't realize it, but you're not gonna believe who our new next-door neighbor is," John Conlogue Sr. said to his family after making the deposit on their new home. "Tom Gola. The basketball player."

Puzzled, John Jr. didn't have the slightest clue whom his father was talking about. The boy did not know much about the National Basketball Association (NBA) or the league's big stars, let alone team records and stats, so the magnitude of his new neighbor's stardom was lost on him.

In August 1959, the Gever family moved from Oxford Circle to Brentwood Park in Somerton. Then ten years old, Larry Gever was looking forward to starting the fifth grade at his new school, Watson Comly Elementary. Attending a new school would help him make new friends in the neighborhood, and, of course, sports would be involved. Gever's favorite sport was basketball.

Prior to the family's move, Gever's father had introduced him to the game, and he had been hooked from the start. Gever practiced his game on the grassy court at Carnell Elementary School, located on Devereaux Avenue in Philadelphia.

The Philadelphia Warriors were Gever's favorite basketball team as he was growing up. However, he would have to beg to go to the games in person at the Philadelphia Civic Center because not all the games were televised. When Gever did get the chance to watch the games, one player in particular caught his eye: Gola. Gever wanted to imitate Gola so badly that when he would play pickup basketball games, he made sure he was the playmaker on the court.

"Tom represented everything that was perfect to me. He was good-looking, strong, really tall for a guard, and, most of all, he could shoot a basketball like hell," Gever says.

In August 1959, Gever and his new friends Mark Creager and Johnny Conlogue were playing stickball in the summer heat. Conlogue mentioned to the crew that Gola lived next door to him in Brentwood Park. When Gever heard the news, he was star struck. He recalls being speechless and feeling his chest pump in excitement.

"We've got to find a way to meet him," Gever said.

They figured there had to be a way to meet Gola—but what was it? Conlogue's father owned a lawn-mowing company and a rotary mower, but the boys knew that their parents wouldn't let three ten-year-olds operate heavy mowing equipment. Their next idea was to knock on Gola's front door, hoping that the basketball player would answer. Finally, they agreed to wait for the first snowfall of the year, when they could offer to shovel Gola's driveway.

During the week of November 21, 1959, Brentwood Park experienced its first snow of the winter. The storm wasn't that big, but it was enough for all three boys to get sent home from school. They rushed off their bus as fast as they could because they knew where they wanted to go: Gola's house. They threw on junky corduroys, mittens, and hats and planned to meet at Conlogue's house. The boys nervously walked down the sidewalk to Gola's home, deciding which one would knock on Gola's door first. Creager was chosen to knock, a simple tap on a wooden door that the three boys had been waiting for months to open. To their disappointment, Caroline Gola answered the door.

"Can I help you boys?" she asked.

"Mrs. Gola? We'd like to shovel Mr. Gola's walkway and sidewalk," one of the boys said. "We would like to do it for free."

"Sure, Tom and I would like to have a clear sidewalk, but you will not do it for free," she replied. "I will pay you $2 each."

In 1959, $6 was a lot of money for shoveling snow. The boys decided that they would just ask for Gola's autograph instead of taking money. They finished the job in under ten minutes and again knocked on the door.

"Could we have Mr. Gola's autograph instead?" one of the boys asked.

"Come in, boys, and have a seat on the sofa. I'll go get Tom," Caroline replied.

After the three friends had nervously waited for a few minutes on the sofa, Gola came into the living room and extended a handshake to them.

"Boys, Caroline tells me you did a fantastic job shoveling the walk," he said. "I'll be glad to give each of you an autograph and $5 apiece for doing such a nice job."

Two months of anticipation came down to this moment. The boys were frozen in their seats, speechless in front of their hero. They couldn't make a sound.

"Sit down, boys, and my wife will bring you some hot chocolate and cookies to warm you up a bit. We can talk," Gola continued.

Gola and the boys spoke about the Warriors, and Gever asked whether Wilt Chamberlain was really as tall as people said.

"You bet he is that tall," Gola replied. "Biggest in the NBA, and we're sure glad we have him on the Warriors."

Caroline brought out cookies and hot chocolate, and the treats were devoured over twenty minutes of conversation. After the snack, Gola asked the boys a very serious question: "Do you boys have plans for this Sunday afternoon?"

He then offered to bring Gever, Conlogue, and Creager to a Sunday afternoon game at the Philadelphia Convention Hall as his guest. The Warriors were playing the Knicks, and the boys could not have been more excited. All three got permission to accompany Gola to the game.

At 10:00 A.M. on Sunday, the boys met at Conlogue's house and walked together to Gola's. They watched him kiss Caroline good-bye and get into his street-parked car, a brand-new Pontiac Bonneville. (At the time, the Bonneville was the most expensive Pontiac, with prices starting between $3,255 and $3,530.) The three scrambled into the back of the Pontiac, and they began their trip to Convention Hall, which was an hour's drive from Somerton. Gola's Pontiac had power windows, which the stunned boys did not know how to use.

Halfway into the trip, Creager suddenly threw up in the backseat. Gola quickly rolled down the windows to air out the car and took a detour to his mother's house at 3rd and Lindley. Gola introduced the boys to his mother and grabbed some paper towels, a scrubbing brush, and a bucket of water to clean the car.

After this brief detour, the boys and Gola continued to the game. Gola parked in the players' parking lot at the back entrance of Convention Hall and then got the boys settled in mid-court seats, three rows from the floor. The Warriors lost the game, 127–126, with Gola scoring 16 points and grabbing 12 rebounds.

Afterward, Gola gave the boys Warriors' game programs autographed by everyone on the team. They got to see Chamberlain, Ernie Beck, and Woody Sauldsberry up close.

That's the kind of person Gola was—a superstar athlete going above and beyond the hopes of three neighborhood kids. It was a day that Gever, Conlogue, and Creager would never forget.

"We couldn't believe our good fortune," Gever says.

Gola treated everyone he encountered with appreciation and decency. Even as his fame grew, he treated people the same. He was appreciative and humbled that people in his neighborhood showed him attention. Gola treated neighborhood kids Gever, Conlogue, and Creager like they mattered. His community impact was his legacy.

. . . .

AS GOLA'S LIFE CONTINUED, he never forgot his roots; he wanted to do right by the schools that had educated him and given him a chance to play basketball. In 1972, Joe Hand Jr. was an eighth grader at Saint Bartholomew School in Northeast Philadelphia. Hand was playing on one of the best middle-school basketball teams in the city at the time, under head coach Tom Gannon. The Saint Bartholomew team was participating in a tournament with other notable Catholic Youth Organization (CYO) schools, including Holy Cross, St. Timothy's, and other local schools. The tournament was held at the La Salle College High School gymnasium.

"It was the grade school tournament [equivalent] of the NCAA [National Collegiate Athletic Association] March Madness," Hand says.

Hand and the Saint Bartholomew team won the basketball tournament. La Salle High School alum Gola served as a special master of ceremonies.

"He just had this certain presence about him when he would walk into a room," Hand recalls.

Gola had the honor of handing out the trophies and the Most Valuable Player (MVP) award for the tournament, which Hand, whose number was 15 like Gola's, received. Hand would later attend La Salle College High School on a scholarship and play basketball at King's College in Wilkes-Barre, Pennsylvania. Although he would not make the final team roster, he was drafted by the Philadelphia 76ers in the tenth round in the 1980 NBA draft. (Hand and his father, Joe Hand Sr., would also found Joe Hand Promotions in 1971, a boxing promoter of pay-per-view and closed-circuit broadcasts of sporting events.)

"He [Gola] always made you feel like you kind of knew him for a really long time, or that if you hadn't seen him in a while, you felt like you just saw him yesterday. That's what I always kind of remember about him—just what a nice man he was," Hand says.

· · · · · · · · ·

EVEN AFTER HIS PROFESSIONAL BASKETBALL CAREER was over, Gola used his political platform and influence to help Dan Walsh, another neighbor, almost ten years later. With help from Gola, Walsh's transition into college in the summer of 1970 was more than memorable—it was life-changing.

Fresh off graduating from Archbishop Ryan High School, Walsh was working as a cashier at the A&P food store on Krewston Road in Northeast Philadelphia. He would encounter various customers on a daily basis, ringing up groceries and starting conversations.

Caroline came into the A&P quite frequently, and the majority of the time, she chose to go through Walsh's checkout line. A friendship developed, and after several visits, the two talked about Walsh's future education plans. Walsh's intentions were to attend community college in the fall, but Caroline thought that her husband could help guide and counsel him toward a better choice.

"I want you to meet my husband," Caroline insisted.

Caroline was proactive. She knew that, through his political network and his knowledge of Philadelphia's educational programs and resources, Gola could help Walsh go in the right direction and get some financial aid. Caroline invited Walsh to their house for dinner, after which Gola vowed to find ways to get Walsh some funding to sustain his education. Money for education was limited for the Walsh family, since Walsh's father, Thomas, had died six years earlier at age fifty-four, just one year after retiring from the Philadelphia Fire Department. Perhaps the son of a police officer recognized something in the son of a firefighter.

"Gola was very instrumental [in] ensuring me funding from the state of Pennsylvania," Walsh says.

Gola was able to see that Walsh was awarded the mayor's scholarship in Philadelphia and the Pennsylvania Higher Education Assistance Agency (PHEAA) scholarship, totaling nearly $5,000 in tuition assistance. But even with this monetary support, Walsh could not afford to live on campus due to his work schedule at the A&P.

Walsh attended Villanova for one semester but ultimately left to follow

Gola's path and join the blue and gold at La Salle. Because of some non-transferable credits, he had to essentially start over, but he ultimately graduated from La Salle in 1974 as an accounting major.

"Tom never held it against me that I wanted to go to Villanova," Walsh says.

While in school, Walsh managed to balance his studies and his financial needs, working forty to fifty hours a week while crafting a schedule of classes on Monday, Wednesday, and Friday. Thanks to his education, Walsh made a career in the healthcare and healthcare information technology (IT) industries. Over the course of nearly forty years, Walsh lost contact with the Golas.

During the Explorers' 2013 NCAA Tournament run, Walsh kept a close eye on his alma mater. As La Salle advanced in the tournament, his heart told him to find a way to visit Gola, who at the time was hospitalized in North Philadelphia at St. Joseph's Manor. Walsh saw how La Salle's past team history was being talked about in the news after almost fifty years and took it as a sign.

In mid-March 2013, instead of going to work one day, Walsh decided to visit Gola at his rehabilitation center in North Philadelphia. He suspected that Gola wouldn't remember him, but he wanted to thank the man who had helped shift his life. On the day of his visit, Walsh brought a poster he had received from the *Philadelphia Daily News*—an acrylic painting by South Jersey artist Stan Kotzen—of Philadelphia sports icons, including Chamberlain, Bobby Clarke, Robin Roberts, and Gola.

Walsh exited the elevator and headed toward Gola's room, only to find a receptionist and nurses asking whether he was another reporter visiting the basketball legend. He assured them he was a close friend. Walsh sat down with Gola for more than an hour, talking about various topics. Although it was a one-sided conversation due to Gola's health, Walsh believed the visit was meant to be.

"It was good to come visit him and thank him for what he did for me," Walsh says.

Walsh showed Gola the poster he had brought with him, and Gola recognized Chamberlain and some other players, as if his memories were awakening. Walsh left the poster in Gola's room before leaving the rehab center. On his way out, he ran into Caroline, completing the reunion.

In 2011, Walsh made a speech at the Mercy Vocational High School commencement ceremony. There, he talked about Gola but didn't mention his name. Instead, he told the crowd of excited seniors not to be afraid to talk to other people in their lives.

"I didn't know he was changing my life at the time," he said in his speech.

Looking back at his own early life, Walsh sees his willingness to reach out to the Golas and theirs to reach back as certainly making a difference. Walsh's history is yet another touched by Gola's legacy.

"He was a man to me that I always felt like he had much more important stature in life than I myself would probably ever receive," he says. "There were moments in my life where I would always look back and say, 'I wouldn't be where I am today if it was not for Tom Gola.'"

· · · · · · · · ·

THE HISTORY of La Salle's men's basketball program certainly stands on Gola's legacy, not just because his playing and coaching brought so many accolades to the school but also because his decision to pass up more prominent programs in favor of the Catholic university in his backyard meant that others would follow in his footsteps. Not even four years after he had left the La Salle basketball program, the big question was who would be the next Gola.

In 1959, Bill Raftery, a senior from Saint Cecilia High School in Kearny, New Jersey, was receiving offers from Catholic schools from around the country, including Holy Cross, Georgetown, Providence, Notre Dame, and others. In the end, Raftery decided to travel ninety-five miles from his hometown to become a La Salle Explorer.

"Tommy had some influence," Raftery says.

Raftery had met Gola at Madison Square Garden while in high school and even had had a chance to speak with him in the locker room after a game. Knowing of Gola's popularity at La Salle and that Donald "Dudey" Moore was coaching the Explorers at the time made Raftery's decision to attend La Salle a little easier.

"He was so accomplished, he made the game look easy. He never looked like he was seeming up or in overdrive, but yet he got there. He was a fluid kind of player," Raftery says.

Raftery started his La Salle career in 1960 on the freshman team, where he quickly broke records, scoring 370 points and averaging 26.4 points per game. *Parade* named him to its All-American freshman team. La Salle basketball fans recognized Raftery's talent and even started describing him as the next coming of Gola.

"That became the joke. We always said [that] each guy that came in was said to be the fiftieth guy to replace Tom Gola. Nobody quite did it like he did it," Raftery recalls.

In his sophomore year, "Mr. Cool," as the La Salle basketball media guide called Raftery, led the team in scoring, with 17.8 points per game and 392 for the season, 8 points away from being only the second player in La Salle's history to score 400 points or more during his sophomore season.

A ruptured disc caused Raftery to miss the majority of the 1962 season; he played in only four games before sitting out the rest of the year. He underwent an operation in January 1962 and was back on the court just in time to play in an alumni game versus Gola and the 1954 NCAA championship team in May.

"That was quite a thrill for all of us," Raftery says.

Raftery's senior year in 1963 coincided with La Salle's centennial celebration. The 1963 team won sixteen games and advanced to the first round of the National Invitation Tournament (NIT), losing to Saint Louis, 63–61. This NIT appearance was the team's first postseason game since Gola's 1955 team had played San Francisco for the NCAA championship.

Although he had only a nominal relationship with Gola, Raftery respects the way he lived his life.

"As a person, humanity comes to mind. He just enjoyed people," Raftery says. "He did it with such ease, comfort, and humility. Everyone felt that they were a friend of his."

To this day, players entering La Salle's basketball program look up to Gola's legacy. Be they NCAA or La Salle team records, Gola set the standards.

. . . .

GOLA'S LEGACY also took another form: players and coaches modeled their games after him and saw his impact on their programs.

Gola's impact on the basketball community even inspired such well-known figures as long-time Texas Tech and Indiana University head basketball coach Bob Knight. His admiration of Gola started back in the 1950s, when he led La Salle to victory in the 1954 NCAA championship.

"I remember listening to the radio game when La Salle won the NCAA Tournament," Knight says.

Knight was playing forward on the Orrville High School basketball team and admired the way Gola played the game.

"All of the kids have favorites in sports, and he was by far my favorite as a kid growing up," Knight recalls.

Over the years, Knight watched and listened to Gola's games whenever he could, but he never got the chance to see him play in person.

"When I had the chance to watch him, I really enjoyed him. I thought he was a great example as to what a basketball player should be. I mean, he did everything. He was a great passer, he scored, he defended, rebounded," he says.

Like Gola, Knight was also a three-sport player in high school, participating in football, baseball, and basketball.

"As a player, I developed a tremendous respect for the way Gola played the game. I think at the time he played, he did everything. He rebounded, he played defense, he scored," Knight says.

After graduating from Orrville High School, Knight attended Ohio State in 1959, where he, Jerry Lucas, and John Havlicek played under Coach Fred Taylor. Knight went on to have a decorated collegiate career as a reserve for the national championship Ohio State team in 1960. His following two seasons ended with Knight's team as the runner-up in the NCAA championship, losing back-to-back tournaments to the Cincinnati Bearcats in 1961 and 1962. After graduating from Ohio State, Knight spent one year as the junior varsity basketball coach at Cuyahoga Falls High School in Ohio. His interest in coaching came from his passion as a player.

Through hundreds of recruiting trips, phone calls, and workouts, Knight always had Gola in the back of his mind—he wanted a duplicate on his team.

"I thought as I coached that was the kind of player that I wanted," Knight says. "A player that could do the things that he did and was a player that could do well at all aspects of the game, not just rebound or score or whatever it might be. I always look for players that can play the game in its entirety. That came from how I learned about the game, watching Gola play."

. . . .

PHILADELPHIA NATIVE MICHAEL BROOKS was no stranger to the game of basketball as a kid, playing in the Sonny Hill basketball league. He attended West Catholic High School, where he received All-Catholic League and All-City honors and broke numerous records, scoring 382 points during his senior year while averaging 27.3 points per game. Brooks scored 1,651 points during his four years at West Catholic, the school's top scoring record. Brooks received basketball scholarship offers from Villanova, La Salle, Memphis State, St. Joseph's, and Rutgers.

Years after his playing and coaching days at La Salle, Gola remained a big asset to the school's athletic family. Whatever the program needed, Gola's assistance was just a phone call away.

Gola would help with the recruiting process from time to time, but Brooks's recruitment was different. Gola had been in his situation thirty years earlier, when multiple schools wanted his services. Gola discussed with Brooks the process of deciding which school to pick.

Brooks could go to a school down south and just be another name in another town, or he could stay in the city where he grew up and ride the wave of Philadelphia basketball.

"I told Mike that all the [Philadelphia] sportswriters knew and respected him," Gola told *Sports Illustrated* in 1980. "And that if he moved to another town, he'd have to convince a lot of other sportswriters that he was a good player."

"When someone like that comes to talk to you, you feel honored," Brooks told *Sports Illustrated* in 1980. "Also, he has a nice Cadillac. When I first met him, I was in shock. He drove me from my high school to the campus and I couldn't say anything. I just sat there in amazement and watched him drive."

Brooks decided to stay in Philadelphia.

During his four years at La Salle, he scored 2,628 points and grabbed 1,372 rebounds, leading the Explorers to the 1978 and 1980 NCAA Tournaments. He broke Gola's school record of 2,461 career points during his senior year in 1980. Similar to Gola, Brooks was named the 1980 National Player of the Year and a First Team All-American during his last year at La Salle, where he averaged 24.1 points and 11.5 rebounds per game. Brooks was also the captain of the 1980 U.S. Olympics basketball team. Brooks is one of five players in the history of the NCAA with at least 2,600 points and 1,300 rebounds (joining Lionel Simmons, Oscar Robertson, Elvin Hayes, and David Robinson).

After his senior year, Brooks was drafted by the San Diego Clippers as the ninth overall pick in the 1980 NBA draft, which also featured Kevin McHale, Andrew Toney, and DaMon "Monti" Davis. Brooks went on to play with the Indiana Pacers in 1986–1987 and for the Denver Nuggets in 1987–1988. He continued to play basketball overseas, in Europe, where he won two French titles. Brooks's number 32 jersey is retired at La Salle and currently hangs in the rafters with Gola's jersey. Brooks passed away on August 22, 2016, in Switzerland at the age of fifty-eight.

. . . .

GOLA WAS AN INSPIRATION to the Philadelphia community and around the country during his collegiate and professional days playing the game he loved. Gola brushed shoulders with Hall of Famers, chatted with mayors and governors, and interacted with college presidents and national leaders. Through all of this, Gola remained humble. He never forgot where he came from, the modest row house at 3rd and Lindley in his hometown of Philadelphia.

18

· · · · · · · ·

A Call from the Hall

TOM GOLA'S EXTRAORDINARY CAREER won him recognition from all corners. Awards, honors, and records are not the only way to measure the prominence of his legacy as an athlete and a person, but they give a taste of his impact.

During his days playing with the Philadelphia Warriors, Gola partnered with Wilson Sporting Goods as a part of the company's football and basketball "Famous Player" autograph sets, paired with Paul Hornung, a long-time National Football League (NFL) running back. Hornung played in the NFL from 1957 to 1966, winning four NFL titles and the first Super Bowl in 1967. The Gola basketball set came with an official-size vinyl-and-rubber-covered ball, a goal, and a net. Gola and Hornung served on the Wilson advisory board. Through his relationship with Wilson, Gola's products were also marketed with those of the American tennis player Jack Kramer, the professional golfer Sam Snead, and the baseball player Ron Santo.

Gola was inducted into the Naismith Memorial Basketball Hall of Fame in Springfield, Massachusetts, on April 26, 1976, in the same class as the former National Basketball Association (NBA) player and coach Bill Sharman, the Notre Dame great Edward "Moose" Krause, and the Temple University head coach Harry "Chief" Litwack. During his time at Temple, from

1952 to 1973, Litwack coached to a 373–193 record. His Temple teams reached the postseason thirteen times, won the National Invitation Tournament (NIT) in 1969, and went to the Final Four of the National Collegiate Athletic Association (NCAA) Tournament in 1956 and in 1958. Gola was introduced into the Hall of Fame by the former Syracuse Nationals player Dolph Schayes.

"He was one of the most underrated players in the game," the late Schayes said.

Schayes had been inducted into the Naismith Memorial Basketball Hall of Fame in 1973, and in 2016, the Philadelphia 76ers retired Schayes's number 4 jersey. Schayes died on December 10, 2015.

"He [Gola] was a tremendous talent," Schayes said.

Thomas (Tommy) Christopher Gola, Gola's son, remembers attending the Hall of Fame ceremony along with a large group of friends and family who had traveled in a large motor coach from Philadelphia to Massachusetts.

"The Hall of Fame was not just a trophy on the wall. It was a ceremony. It was an event. It was with a lot of real people. That's when you sit there and say, 'Yeah, boom, he did it,'" Tommy recalls.

Tommy attended middle school at Saint Albert the Great Catholic School in Huntington Valley, Pennsylvania, and then La Salle College High School. He had the opportunity to go to La Salle College but instead went to Widener University for his bachelor's degree. He played basketball throughout his life, but it never got to a point where he wanted to pursue the sport as a career. His father never pressured his son to play the game.

"People expected me to be really good, and I wasn't. I never expected to be, nor did I ever try to be. I just enjoyed the game. What I liked more about it was the whole history of it following him. It just came natural[ly] to dribble a basketball around," Tommy says.

In 1980, Gola received the Silver Anniversary Award from the NCAA in recognition of the twenty-fifth anniversary of the end of his intercollegiate athletic eligibility. The basketball players John "Jack" Twyman, from the University of Cincinnati, and Richard "Dick" Boushka, from Saint Louis University, also received the award that year. Gola is the only La Salle player to date to have received the Silver Anniversary Award and is the third alumnus of a Big 5 school to do so (Marty Liquori, Villanova cross-country/indoor and outdoor track, and Richard Censits, University of Pennsylvania basketball, are the other two).

Gola's name was forever enshrined on the campus at 20th and Olney in 1998, when La Salle dedicated the "Tom Gola Arena." The dedication was made possible by an anonymous La Salle alumnus who donated $200,000. During the 1989–1990 to 1995–1996 seasons, the La Salle basketball teams had played their home games at the Civic Center in downtown Philadelphia. La Salle then played two seasons at the Spectrum before breaking ground on the new expansion and renovation of Hayman Hall, La Salle's gym and arena. The expansion increased the seating capacity of the arena from one thousand seats to four thousand. The total cost of the new project was $6.3 million.

"I was somewhat skeptical and taken back by the thought," Gola told the *Philadelphia Daily News* in September 1998. "When it became a reality, it leaves you kind of speechless. It really is quite an honor."

Ed Rendell, the mayor of Philadelphia, proclaimed "Tom Gola Day" in the city as the Explorers faced Howard University on November 21, 1998.

"Tom Gola taught us lessons about things such as teamwork and leadership on the court," said Rendell in a statement in 1998. "He used the same principles in his professional life: teamwork, bringing people together, reaching out to others. We are enormously proud of him as a basketball player, as a civic leader, and as a businessman. Tom Gola is one of the best sons the city of Philadelphia has ever produced and he has been a champion at every endeavor he undertook."

At the dedication, Gola took to the center of the court to thank the fans for their support.

"I want all of you to support La Salle," he told the crowd. "Because we are coming back."

Gola's name remains in the spotlight during national television broadcast games at Tom Gola Arena.

"If there is no Tom Gola, there is no La Salle," says Bill DeMarco, a member of Gola's political team.

Gola will forever hold the NCAA Division I rebounding record, with 2,201. Joe Holup, a forward who played at George Washington University from 1952 to 1956, holds second place, with 2,030 rebounds.

"That's one of those records that does not have a chance of being broken," says Dick Jerardi, a long-time columnist for the *Philadelphia Daily News*. "The thing about Tom was that he was not a center. He played every position."

With the current length of the NCAA basketball season, a player would have to play for a collegiate team well into the postseason and average more than 20 rebounds per game for four years. The probability of a player of that nature making it past one year at his university and not entering the NBA is highly unlikely.

"Nobody is going break that record for rebounds. That's one thing you can say," says Herb Magee, a long-time coach at Jefferson University (which formed following a merger of Philadelphia University and Thomas Jefferson University).

In the summer of 2001, Gola and the La Salle Athletic Department got in a confrontation that resulted in Gola's removing his 1954 basketball jersey and donating it to the Naismith Memorial Basketball Hall of Fame in Springfield, Massachusetts. Gola told the *Philadelphia Daily News* that he removed the jersey after learning that the university was planning to auction some of the memorabilia that used to hang in William "Speedy" Morris's office as part of an athletics fund raiser. The university disputed this allegation. Gola and La Salle's high-level officials did not speak for an extended period, but the conflict was later resolved.

In 2002, Madison Square Garden's Holiday Festival Tournament celebrated its fiftieth anniversary by selecting the five greatest players in its history. Receiving the honors were Gola, Bill Bradley (Princeton), Oscar Robertson (Cincinnati), Chris Mullin (St. John's), and Kareem Abdul-Jabbar (UCLA).

"He was huge in New York City. He was huge in the Garden," says Dick Weiss, a long-time college and professional basketball writer for the *Philadelphia Daily News* and New York's *Daily News*.

Gola has also been inducted into the following Halls of Fame: Helms College Basketball, Northeast Philadelphia, Archdiocese of Philadelphia Catholic Youth Organization (CYO), Philadelphia Sports, and Polish Hall of Fame. Gola was offered a place in the Italian Hall of Fame, but officials withdrew the offer after finding out that he was not Italian. Although he never competed in the Atlantic 10 Conference basketball tournament, Gola was inducted into the Atlantic 10 Legends Inaugural Class of 2013. The conference was formed in 1975 and was known as the Eastern Collegiate Basketball League and the Eastern 8 until changing its name to the Atlantic 10 in 1982; La Salle University would join the league in 1995.

19

. . . .

Gola at Work and
at Home

OUTSIDE HIS FAMOUS PURSUITS of basketball and politics, Tom Gola made his mark on the Philadelphia region as a businessman. His tenure in professional basketball gave him and his family the finances to invest in business ventures. When Gola was home, he was a family man, partaking in hunting, golf, and other sports activities.

In 1959, during the height of his career with the Warriors, Gola launched a company he named the Tom Gola Driving Range. He had two locations, one on the Roosevelt Boulevard in the Somerton section of Philadelphia and the other in the Roxborough section.

Golf would be a fixture for Gola throughout his life, during and after his National Basketball Association (NBA) career. Every Saturday found him on a golf course, playing a round of eighteen holes with a cigar in his mouth. Gola and his friends would frequently play at various courses throughout Pennsylvania, including Sandy Run Country Club, Squires Golf Club, and Whitford Country Club. Gola played with long-time friends from Incarnation and other friends and family.

"He was like another father to me. He always invited me to any kind of golf outings he had," says Garry Gola, Gola's nephew.

Gola's image as a basketball star led him to a unique business opportunity as a spokesperson. During his playing days with the Knicks in the

1960s, Gola was asked to appear in a commercial for Vitalis, for which he was paid $2,500. Gola also became a member of the Screen Actors Guild for appearing in the ad.

"He didn't even speak," Caroline Gola laughs.

In 1967, a couple of years into his tenure as a state representative, Gola founded the Thomas J. Gola Insurance Agency in Fort Washington, Pennsylvania, specializing in fire and casualty insurance. He would later sell the company.

Gola invested in rental properties in the late 1960s, owning and managing two apartment complexes in the Olney and Frankford sections of Northeast Philadelphia.

After losing his city controller position in the 1974 election, Gola opened and managed an ice-skating rink on Roosevelt Boulevard in North Philadelphia with Lou Anges, his friend and a Philadelphia contractor. Anges and his crew built the rink from the ground up. Gola thought that the North Philadelphia area needed a nice attraction in the neighborhood to drive local business, and the basketball star wanted to experiment with skates and ice.

In January 1974, Gola was rumored to be considered for the general manager position with the Philadelphia 76ers following the departure of Don DeJardin the previous fall. Gola and Irv Kosloff, the owner of the Philadelphia 76ers, had a meeting, but nothing ever came to fruition. If Gola had joined the team, he would have worked with head coach Gene Shue and players Fred Carter, Tom Van Arsdale, Steve Mia, Doug Collins, and others.

In 1975, Gola was the president of the G and S Company, a landfill business in the Philadelphia metropolitan area. The city of Philadelphia would later purchase the company.

Gola got involved in politics again in 1980, helping Ronald Reagan in his bid for the White House by serving as the Philadelphia chair of the campaign. The following year, he was named a regional administrator for the U.S. Department of Housing and Urban Development, where he worked for two years.

After his failed mayoral run in 1983, Gola went on to become a successful executive, serving as the vice president of Valley Forge Investment Corporation. The company was owned and operated by Richard Ireland, a long-time friend, an Olney native, and a graduate of Northeast Catholic

High School and La Salle College. Over the years, Gola worked closely with Richard and his son, Jon, at their offices in King of Prussia, Pennsylvania.

"I treasured . . . my relationship with him. Every minute of it. It was fabulous. The memories are the greatest in the world," recalls Jon.

At Valley Forge Investment Corporation, Gola worked closely with medical waste companies, hotel divisions, and commercial real estate properties with clients from Massachusetts to Virginia and as far west as Ohio.

"Tom wasn't just a good jock. He was a bright businessman," says Jon.

Gola helped the Irelands' company secure large business opportunities, offering access to his Rolodex of other business professionals and political leaders throughout the Delaware Valley. Gola was ahead of the curve in business deals. He always knew who could smooth things out.

"Tom Gola is the only person that I know to call the White House and get a response," Jon Ireland says.

Jon looked up to Gola as he would an uncle or a second father. The Ireland family would occasionally take Gola hunting for white-tailed deer on their two-hundred-acre farm in South Coatesville, Pennsylvania. The farm location was called "Wildwoods," a tribute to Richard's childhood at the beach in Wildwood, New Jersey, where Gola, coincidentally, had also spent his summers. One time, the Irelands and Gola went hunting on the property with former University of Pennsylvania football player Ed Allen, former Boston College quarterback Doug Guyer, and former Philadelphia Eagles coach and Super Bowl XXXIV champion Dick Vermeil.

The Golas and the Irelands were a close-knit group, so much so that Jon gave Gola his brown and white Jack Russell terrier. The dog, which Gola renamed "1–5" after his jersey number, was not the friendliest animal. The Golas loved animals and even at one point kept racehorses and ponies on their thirteen-acre home in North Philadelphia. For his son's sixth birthday, Gola bought two ponies, naming them Honey and Coaltown.

Gola told the *Philadelphia Bulletin* in 1979, "I like horses a lot more than politics. Horses make a lot more money. And they don't talk."

When Gola was away from the spotlight of basketball, politics, and business, he enjoyed listening to jazz music, particularly that of Stan Kenton and John Coltrane. One of his favorite songs was Neil Diamond's "Sweet Caroline," which he sang to his wife. Among Gola's lesser-known talents, according to Caroline, was a flair for writing.

"Tom lost his calling," Caroline says. "He would have been a tremendous writer. He had that talent for a pen and a paper."

In July 2003, Gola suffered a head injury outside a restaurant and was rushed to the University of Pennsylvania. Gola and Caroline were with two other couples when he lost his balance and fell backward, hitting his head on the curb. Gola spent time in and out of Holy Redeemer St. Joseph Manor in Meadowbrook, Pennsylvania.

Caroline decorated her husband's room with sports memorabilia: photos, hats, letters, clothing. She hung a poster of a Stan Kotzen acrylic painting made for the *Philadelphia Daily News*, a gift from their old neighbor Dan Walsh, that depicted Philadelphia players of the century, including Phillies pitcher Robin Roberts and center fielder Richie Ashburn, Flyers center Bob Clarke, and, of course, Gola.

Next to Gola's dresser was a 7-by-10-inch photo of Gola and Wilt Chamberlain, who had signed it "The Big Dipper." Gola had played with the 7-ft. superstar for the Warriors from 1959 until Gola was traded in 1962. "If you only passed more often, I could have scored 100 a couple more times," Chamberlain had written in a postscript on the photo.

"When I was growing up, you whispered the name Tom Gola, because he was like a saint," Chamberlain once said.

While Gola was in the hospital, fans still wrote to request his autograph.

"Although I did not get to see you play, my dad has told me about your wonderful career," one fan wrote.

Because Gola's health left him unable to write, Caroline answered the fan mail, but she refused to sign his name—she couldn't take credit, she said, for what he had accomplished.

With Caroline, family, and friends by his side, Gola passed away on January 26, 2014, at the age of eighty-one.

"Tom was a Philadelphia icon whose name is synonymous with basketball," said Brother Michael J. McGinniss, La Salle's president for fifteen years, at the time of Gola's death. "His legacy will live on at La Salle forever and in the University's Tom Gola Arena."

Following his death, the NCAA tweeted a statement: "Thoughts to the family/friends of Tom Gola, as well as entire La Salle University community. Gola was among best in college basketball's history. #legend." The 2013–

2014 La Salle men's basketball team honored Gola by wearing a memorial "15" patch on their jerseys for the remainder of the season.

"Tom Gola is known by all as a truly great player and coach, but it was the man that was most cherished at La Salle. Every person connected with La Salle basketball for over a sixty-year span has held his friendship and leadership as a blessing they could always count on," said John Giannini, La Salle's head coach at the time of Gola's death.

"On behalf of the entire Philadelphia 76ers organization, we are deeply saddened to learn of the unfortunate passing of La Salle basketball legend Tom Gola," said Scott O'Neil, 76ers chief executive officer. "Tom will always be fondly remembered for his dedication to this city and as an icon for his accomplishments both on and off the court."

A year after Gola's death, on January 25, 2015, the La Salle Athletic Department unveiled a statue in his honor in the Hayman Center. The statue was created by the artist Chad Fisher, of Fisher Sculpture LLC.

In April 2017, La Salle University announced that it had sold the naming rights to its arena to TruMark Financial Credit Union. The arena also kept Gola's name, so it is now officially known as Tom Gola Arena at TruMark Financial Center.

Today, Caroline is the proud keeper of her husband's basketball legacy. She lives in the same house that Gola built for the family in 1982. The trophy room in the house is still full, and more memorabilia fills a closet. Caroline still has her husband's old jerseys, including his college All-Star game jersey and a complete Philadelphia Warriors red, blue, and gold warm-up suit with pants and the limited-edition jacket.

Gola's name is always mentioned as one of the all-time greats. He was a true professional who paved the way for basketball in Philadelphia. Gola lived a prodigious life through basketball, coaching, and politics, doing so in the city where he grew up. Gola is and forever will be associated with Philadelphia. Throughout every obstacle and chapter in his life, he was Mr. All-Around.

·········

Acknowledgments

ALTHOUGH MY NAME GRACES the cover of this book, it would not have come to fruition without the help of many others along the way.

I thank my best friend and wife, Jodi, for pushing me to finish the manuscript. I thank the man above for bringing us together during our freshman year at La Salle University, in 2009; we have not looked back since.

I am grateful to the extended Grzybowski family—my parents, Danny and Joanna; my brothers, Johnathan and Jeffrey; Uncle John; and the Gilbert family—for their love and support. I am indebted to my best friend, Andrew Groy, for always driving me to work hard.

My deepest thanks go to Caroline Gola for opening her door to me and for allowing me to tell the story of her husband's life on and off the court. I thoroughly enjoyed each of our conversations. I hope this book reflects the remarkable life that Tom lived.

My research for this book began at La Salle University, in the basement of College Hall, at the university archives office, with the help of Brother Joseph Grabenstein. "Someone should write a book about Tom Gola," he said. I took these words to heart, and here we are, years later, with the completed biography in hand. I thank Brother Joe for his friendship and guidance throughout the project—this book would not have become a reality without him. La Salle is fortunate to have benefited from his service all these years. Every university needs and deserves a Brother Joe in its Archives Department. I also thank Rebecca Goldman and Katie Carey of the La Salle University Archives Department for their considerable help.

I am grateful to Ryan Mulligan and the Temple University Press team. I can't count the many times I e-mailed and called Ryan to bug him with questions about the manuscript. I truly could not have turned my manuscript into a book without him. I also offer special thanks to the rest of the Temple University Press team: Aaron Javsicas, Nikki Miller, Gary Kramer, Ann-Marie Anderson, Kate Nichols, and Joan Vidal. Special thanks go to copyeditor Heather Wilcox for her hard work on this book.

I am much obliged to Tom's brothers, John and Paul "Mo" Gola, for telling me extraordinary stories of Tom's past, and to Tom's son, Thomas Gola, for sharing his many memories and insights. I thank them all for their support of this book.

I owe special thanks to Brenda Galloway-Wright and Josué Hurtado at Temple University Libraries and Special Collections Research Center for facilitating my research and photo acquisition. I also thank Jaimie Korelitz of Getty Images for helping me procure the photo for the front cover of this book.

I am grateful to Bill Raftery for writing the Foreword, and I tip my hat to Bill's daughter, Suzi Herbst, for her assistance.

I thank my La Salle family, Dr. Colleen Hanycz and Bill Bradshaw, as well as Albert "Scooter" Vertino, Dan Lobacz, Kale Beers, Kevin Bonner, Joe Meade, Beth Salazar, and Brother Gerry Molyneaux.

I am indebted to the long-time *Philadelphia Daily News* scoreboard editor Bob Vetrone Jr. for assisting with research and for reading drafts of several chapters. Whenever I had a question or needed anything, he was quick to help. I thank the *Philadelphia Inquirer* writer and proud La Salle alumnus Mike Sielski for his advice, support, and guidance throughout the writing process.

Special thanks go to my good friend Andrew Albert for editing one of the first versions of this book. I greatly appreciate his support and friendship.

I am grateful to Jared Caracciolo, Pat McClone, Bernard Schneider, Frank Daily, Dennis Fiandra, and Eddie Altieri for their assistance at every stage.

Finally, I thank the many people who graciously took time out of their busy schedules to answer questions pertaining to this book, especially Frank Blatcher, Jack Moore, Eddie Altieri, Charlie Greenberg, Fran O'Malley, Al Cantello, Ernie Beck, Curt Fromal, "Speedy" Morris, Roland Taylor, Larry Cannon, Fran Dunphy, John Chaney, Shanin Specter, Sonny Hill, Dick Jerardi, Bobby Knight, Herb Magee, Dick Weiss, Bob Pettit, Tommy Heinsohn, Jerry Lucas, Harvey Pollack, and Lionel Simmons. I hope I did all their stories justice.

Appendix 1

Correspondence

The White House
Washington

June 21, 1955

Dear Mr Gola—

You undoubtedly know of the increasing concern that too many of our young people are spectators rather than active participants in athletic events. It has been suggested to me that, at an informal luncheon meeting of representatives of the sports world, ways might be developed to counteract this trend and to induce young people to participate more actively in sports. Thereby the physical fitness of our American people would be improved and juvenile delinquency reduced.

Would it be possible for you to attend such a luncheon that I am planning for Monday, July eleventh, at half past twelve, at the White House?

With best wishes,

Sincerely,

President Dwight D. Eisenhower

Voice of America
United States Information Agency
Washington

September 9, 1955

Mr. Tom Gola
La Salle College
Philadelphia, Pennsylvania

Dear Mr. Gola:

On Thursday evening, 9 September 1955 at 8:30P.M. E.D.T., the Voice of America on its regular English transmission to Latin America, broadcast the interview which you were kind enough to record for us upon your return from an extended tour of that area of the world.

On behalf of our organization and also personally, I should like to take this opportunity to thank you and assure you that you have made a contribution to Inter-American understanding and goodwill. Your Department of State–sponsored tour and the following up broadcast were both in the best tradition of extending a helping hand to our neighbors to the south in a friendly, unpatronizing manner. In the manner you are best qualified, you have aided in cementing the friendly ties among our countries of the Americas. Sports activities have sometimes been called the universal meeting ground for peoples of various races, creeds and nationalities. The excellent reception accorded your visit reiterated this policy.

I have communicated with the Honorable Joseph Clark, Mayor of the City of Philadelphia, and a copy of the letter is enclosed. Also, a tape recording of the interview has been sent to Mr. Frederick Walker of television station WPTZ for possible use on the air locally.

Thank you once again for your cooperation and the very best of good luck to you and your charming wife.

Very truly yours,

Robert J. Kent
Worldwide English Branch
Voice of America
Washington, D.C.

City of Philadelphia
Frank L. Rizzo
Mayor

November 7, 1973

Honorable Tom Gola
City Controller
Room 1230 Municipal Services Building
Philadelphia, Penna. 19107

Dear Tom,

I know that words can't express the full depth of my sorrow over your defeat.

But even in defeat, we manage sometimes to come up with an even better outlook. In your case, with your great talent and your youth, there are no horizons that you can't reach, and if I can help in any way, you can depend on me.

Sincerely,

Frank L. Rizzo

Appendix 2

Statistics

La Salle College Playing Record

1952: Freshman Year

29 games played
Points per Game (PPG): 17.4
Points: 505
Rebounds: 497
Rebounds per Game (RPG): 17.1

Freshman Year Honors
Associated Press (AP) All–National Invitation Tournament (NIT) First Team
AP All-State First Team
National Collegiate Athletic Association (NCAA) All–District II Honorable
    Mention
1952 NIT Most Valuable Player (MVP) Award (shared with Norm Grekin of
    La Salle)
Philadelphia Sports Writers Association All-City First Team
United Press International (UPI) All-NIT First Team

1953: Sophomore Year

28 games played
PPG: 18.5
Points: 517

Rebounds: 434
RPG: 15.5

Sophomore Year Honors
AP All-East First Team
AP All-State First Team
International News Service All-State First Team
Madison Square Garden Holiday Festival MVP
NCAA All–District II First Team
Philadelphia Sports Writers Association All-City First Team
Robert V. Geasey Award (bestowed by the Philadelphia Sports Writers
    Association to the nation's outstanding college basketball player; award
    shared with Ernie Beck of the University of Pennsylvania)
UPI All-East First Team
UPI All-NIT First Team
UPI All-State First Team

1954: Junior Year

30 games played
PPG: 23
Points: 690
Rebounds: 652
RPG: 21.7

Junior Year Honors
Amateur Athletic Union James E. Sullivan Memorial Award nominee (finished
    third in the balloting)
America's Outstanding Athlete for 1954 (named by the Philadelphia Sports
    Writers Association)
AP All-East First Team
AP All-State First Team
Dell Publications College Basketball Player of the Year
Helms Foundation College Basketball Player of the Year
International News Service All-State First Team
NCAA All–District II First Team
NCAA Eastern Regional All-Tournament Team
NCAA Eastern Regional Tournament MVP
NCAA Tournament Final MVP
Philadelphia Sports Writers Association All-City First Team
Robert V. Geasey Award
Sports Magazine College Basketball Player of the Year
UPI All-East First Team
UPI All-State First Team

1955: Senior Year

31 games played
PPG: 24.1
Points: 750
Rebounds: 618
RPG: 19.9

Senior Year Honors
AP All-East First Team
AP All-State First Team
NCAA All–District II First Team
NCAA Eastern Regional MVP
Philadelphia Sports Writers Association All-City First Team
Robert V. Geasey Award
UPI All-East First Team

Totals

Points: 2,462
Rebounds: 2,201

La Salle College Team Performance

1952: NIT Champion
25–7
1953: NIT Quarterfinalist
25–3
1954: NCAA Champion
26–4
1955: NCAA Finalist
26–5
Four-Year Record: 102–19

Professional Basketball Record

1956–1962 Philadelphia Warriors
1963 San Francisco Warriors, New York Knickerbockers
1964–1966 New York Knickerbockers

NBA Total Career Statistics

Years played: 10
Games played: 698
Points: 7,871

PPG: 11.3
Rebounds: 5,605
RPG: 8
Assists: 2,953
Assists per Game (APG): 4.2
All-Star Selections
1960 Philadelphia Warriors
1961 Philadelphia Warriors
1962 Philadelphia Warriors (missed game due to injury)
1963 San Francisco Warriors, New York Knickerbockers
1964 New York Knickerbockers

All-Star Game Career Statistics

Games played: 4
PPG: 7.3
Points: 29
Rebounds: 11
RPG: 2.8

Play-Off Game Career Statistics

Games played: 39
PPG: 11.1
Points: 432
Rebounds: 391
RPG: 10
Assists: 179
APG: 4.6

La Salle College Coaching Record

1969
Record: 23–1
1970
Record: 14–12
Total: 37–13
PCT: .740

Coaching Honors

1969 AP College Coach of the Year (national runner-up)
1969 *Coach and Athlete* College Coach of the Year
1969 New York Metropolitan Basketball Writers Association College Coach
    of the Year

1969 Philadelphia Jewish Basketball League Alumni Man of the Year
1969 Philadelphia Sports Writers Association College Coach of the Year

Hall of Fame Memberships

1957 Helms Foundation College Basketball Hall of Fame
1961 La Salle College Hall of Athletics
1967 Madison Square Garden Basketball Hall of Fame
1968 Pennsylvania Sports Hall of Fame
1976 Naismith Memorial Basketball Hall of Fame
1976 Polish National Hall of Fame

Sources

Books

Auerbach, Red, and John Feinstein. *Let Me Tell You a Story: A Lifetime in the Game.* New York: Back Bay Books, 2005.

Bird, Kai, and René Ruiz. *The Good Spy: The Life and Death of Robert Ames.* New York: Random House Audio, 2014.

Chamberlain, Wilt, and David Shaw. *Wilt: Just Like Any Other 7-Foot Black Millionaire Who Lives Next Door.* New York: Warner Communications, 1975.

Clayton, Skip. *Philadelphia's Big Five: Celebrating the City of Brotherly Love's Basketball Tradition.* New York: Sports Publishing, 2016.

Cunningham, Carson. *American Hoops: U.S. Men's Olympic Basketball from Berlin to Beijing.* Lincoln: University of Nebraska Press, 2009.

Goudsouzian, Aram. *King of the Court: Bill Russell and the Basketball Revolution.* Berkeley: University of California Press, 2011.

Johnson, Scott Morrow. *Phog: The Most Influential Man in Basketball.* Lincoln: University of Nebraska Press, 2016.

Loeffler, Ken. *Ken Loeffler on Basketball.* Englewood Cliffs, NJ: Prentice-Hall, 1955.

Lyons, Robert S. *Palestra Pandemonium: A History of the Big 5.* Philadelphia: Temple University Press, 2002.

Pomerantz, Gary M. *Wilt, 1962: The Night of 100 Points and the Dawn of a New Era.* New York: Three Rivers Press, 2006.

Newspaper Articles

"Alumnus-Owned Firm Paid Players." *La Salle Collegian* (Philadelphia), November 1, 1968.

Brady, Frank. "Tom Gola Gets La Salle Vote." *Philadelphia Bulletin*, August 15, 1968.

Delaney, Ed. "A Night Belongs to Gola and It's about Time." *Philadelphia Inquirer*, March 26, 1956.

Dell, John. "Gola Leaves La Salle, Recommends Fromal." *Philadelphia Inquirer*, February 14, 1970.

———. "Gola Signs Four-Year Pact." *Philadelphia Inquirer*, August 15, 1968.

———. "Gottlieb Says Warriors Will Present Bonus to All on Championship Team." *Philadelphia Inquirer*, April 9, 1956.

Dienna, Nick. "Explorers Win as 'Hot Rod' Sputters: Tigers Are Tame and Griffins Are Caged." *La Salle Collegian* (Philadelphia), March 16, 1955.

———. "Jim Pollard New Cage Mentor; Accepts Three-Year Contract." *La Salle Collegian* (Philadelphia), April 20, 1955.

DiStefano, Jim. "Gola, God, and 17-1 Take on Villanova." *La Salle Collegian* (Philadelphia), February 7, 1969.

———. "Gola to Remain as Coach despite New Job." *La Salle Collegian* (Philadelphia), November 11, 1969.

Dolson, Frank. "Tom Comes Home as Image-Builder." *Philadelphia Daily News*, August 15, 1968.

Gola, Tom. "Gola Tells Why He Fouls as Pro." *Philadelphia Bulletin*, December 28, 1955.

———. "My First Coach." *Parade*, January 29, 1956.

"Gola Forgets Football; Says He's Not in Shape." *Philadelphia Inquirer*, July 26, 1962.

"Gola Is Vote-Getter as a Pennsylvania Legislator and Coach of La Salle's Five." *New York Times*, February 23, 1969.

"Gola Leads Corps of New Coaches." *La Salle Collegian* (Philadelphia), September 17, 1968.

"Gola Rookie in New Game." *Philadelphia Daily News*, January 5, 1967.

"Gola Sworn as Controller; Vows to Keep Spending Honest." *Philadelphia Inquirer*, January 5, 1970.

"Gola to Resign as Coach of La Salle College." *Philadelphia Evening Bulletin*, February 13, 1970.

Goldaper, Sam. "The Gola Campaigns: An End and a Beginning." *New York Herald Tribune*, March 18, 1966.

Good, Herb. "La Salle Defeats Iowa, 76–73, to Gain Final." *Philadelphia Inquirer*, March 18, 1955.

———. "USF Whips La Salle for NCAA Title." *Philadelphia Inquirer*, March 20, 1955.

Greway, Jim. "Gola Brings Optimism to La Salle Campus." *La Salle Collegian* (Philadelphia), September 27, 1968.

Hall, Bill. "O'Brien Calls Tom Gola 'Best I Ever Coached.'" *Philadelphia Bulletin*, April 17, 1959.

Heaney, Jim. "Phase Two: The Tom Gola Era." *La Salle Collegian* (Philadelphia), December 6, 1968.

Heffernan, Jim. "Gola Joins Eagles in Effort to Win Job in Football." *Philadelphia Bulletin*, July 20, 1962.

Hochman, Stan. "Tom's Goal: A Return to Glory." *Philadelphia Daily News*, August 15, 1968.

"Loeffler, Gola to Tour So. America in Summer." *Philadelphia Bulletin*, February 17, 1955.

Lyon, Bill. "Tom Gola Honored, in Arena of His Name." *Philadelphia Inquirer*, November 22, 1998.

McKelvey, Gerald. "Gola to Coach at La Salle, Take Second Shot at Legislature." *Philadelphia Inquirer*, August 25, 1968.

"National Invitation Tourney Gets Fast Start at Garden." *Gettysburg Times*, March 10, 1953.

Richman, Alan. "76ers' New GM? Gola Says Not He." *Philadelphia Bulletin*, December 14, 1973.

Ryan, Jack. "O'Brien Swayed Gola from Football and Baseball." *Philadelphia Bulletin*, February 27, 1955.

"Tom Gola Makes Debut as Warrior." *Philadelphia Bulletin*, October 10, 1955.

Vetrone, Bob. "All-American Fits Tom Gola to a T, College Coaches and Players Agree." *Philadelphia Bulletin*, December 26, 1954.

———. "Gola Family Could Floor Own Team." *Philadelphia Bulletin*, May 11, 1952.

———. "Gola Signs Warriors' Pact at Salary Near $12,000." *Philadelphia Bulletin*, October 7, 1955.

———. "Loeffler's Legacy: Honesty, Victory." *Philadelphia Bulletin*, January 3, 1975.

Online Articles

"The Big Surprise of 1955." *Sports Illustrated*, March 28, 1955. Available at https://www.si.com/vault/1955/03/28/601407/the-big-surprise-of-1955. Accessed October 12, 2017.

Blinebury, Fran. "Philly Hoops Scene Wouldn't Be What It Is without Hill." *NBA.com*, February 18, 2015. Available at http://www.nba.com/2015/news/features/fran_blinebury/02/18/barrier-breakers-sonny-hill/. Accessed January 10, 2018.

Douchant, Mike. "NIT Historical Facts." *USA Today*, March 25, 2002. Available at http://usatoday30.usatoday.com/sports/college/basketball/men/02tourney/nit-tidbits.htm. Accessed April 26, 2018.

"Ex–La Salle, NBA Star Tom Gola, 81, Dies." *NBA.com*, January 27, 2014. Available at http://www.nba.com/2014/news/01/26/tom-gola-la-salle-obit/. Accessed January 10, 2018.

Fitzpatrick, Frank. "Frank's Place: Big 5's Forgotten Coaching Great, Ken Loeffler." *Philly.com*, November 20, 2016. Available at http://www.philly.com/philly/sports/20161120_Frank_s_Place__Big_5_s_forgotten_coaching_great__Ken_Loeffler.html. Accessed October 12, 2017.

Goldstein, Joe. "Explosion: 1951 Scandals Threaten College Hoops." *ESPN.com*, November 19, 2003. Available at https://www.espn.com/classic/s/basketball_scandals_explosion.html. Accessed October 12, 2017.

Hunt, Donald. "Alonzo Lewis Left Lasting Legacy." *Philadelphia Tribune*, February 24, 2012. Available at http://www.phillytrib.com/sports/baseball/alonzo-lewis-left-lasting-legacy/article_c16609d8-d4f9-573f-8343-beb710c204d2.html. Accessed January 10, 2018.

Jackson, Roger. "He Has Reached the Gola." *Sports Illustrated*, January 7, 1980. Available at https://www.si.com/vault/1980/01/07/824275/he-has-reached-the-gola-until-recently-michael-brooks-was-overshadowed-at-la-salle-by-famed-alumnus-tom-gola-but-as-he-zeroes-in-on-golas-records-he-has-built-a-rep-of-his-own. Accessed October 9, 2017.

Kirkpatrick, Curry. "On Top with No Place to Go." *Sports Illustrated*, February 17, 1969. Available at https://www.si.com/vault/1969/02/17/559639/on-top-with-no-place-to-go#. Accessed October 9, 2017.

"La Salle Legend and All-Time NCAA Rebound Leader Tom Gola Dies at 81." *SI.com*, January 27, 2014. Available at https://www.si.com/college-basketball/one-and-one/2014/01/27/la-salle-legend-tom-gola-dies-at-81. Accessed January 10, 2018.

"1951 North-South Cage Classic." Available at http://www.bigbluehistory.net/bb/NorthSouth/1951.html. Accessed January 10, 2018.

"North-South All-Star Game and the Chuck Taylor All-Star Team." Available at http://www.bigbluehistory.net/bb/north-south_frame.html. Accessed April 26, 2018.

Robertson, Oscar. "The Dream Team You've Never Heard Of." *The Undefeated*, August 11, 2016. Available at https://theundefeated.com/features/the-dream-team-youve-never-heard-of/. Accessed October 9, 2017.

Ronaldson, Tim. "Gola Honored as Atlantic 10 Basketball Legend." *Northeast Times*, March 20, 2013. Available at https://northeasttimes.com/gola-honored-as-atlantic-10-basketball-legend-40584274d743. Accessed January 10, 2018.

Story, Mark. "The First Kentucky Wildcats to Go 25-0 Were No Slouches, Either." *Kentucky Sports*, February 14, 2015. Available at http://www.kentucky.com/sports/college/kentucky-sports/uk-basketball-men/article44554212.html. Accessed January 10, 2018.

Twyman, Lisa. "The Last Word in P.A. Announcers Is Pronounced Daaaave Ziiiink-Offff!" *Sports Illustrated*, March 12, 1984. Available at https://www.si.com/vault/1984/03/12/569079/the-last-word-in-p-a-announcers-is-pronounced-daaaave-ziiiinkoffff. Accessed October 12, 2017.

Magazines

Bilovsky, Frank. "An All-American for the Ages." *La Salle Magazine*, Winter 1998–1999.

———. "The Birth of the Big 5." *La Salle Magazine*, Winter 1996–1997.

Lyons, Robert. "The Closest Thing to the Irreplaceable Man." *La Salle Magazine*, Spring 1987.

———. "Diary of a Long Distance Leaper: Ira Davis, Who Competed in Three Olympic Games, Sits on the Threshold of Perhaps His Greatest Triumph." *La Salle Magazine*, Spring 1990.

———. "Everybody Relied on His Wisdom." *La Salle Magazine*, Summer 1983.

McCormick, Bernard. "The Heavy-Hitting Surgeon: Hank DeVincent Has Spent His Career Repaying a Longstanding Debt to the Christian Brothers." *La Salle Magazine*, Fall 1989.

———. "'I Can See Tom Gola Now . . .' The Year the Explorers Won the NCAA Basketball Championship." *La Salle Magazine*, Winter 1994–1995.

Vetrone, Bob. "A Championship Season." *La Salle Magazine*, Winter 1991–1992.

Media Guides

La Salle College Basketball Handbook 1950–1951.
La Salle College Basketball Handbook 1951–1952.
La Salle College Basketball Handbook 1952–1953.
La Salle College Basketball Handbook 1954–1955.
La Salle College Basketball Handbook 1955–1956.
La Salle College Basketball Handbook 1968–1969.
La Salle College Basketball Handbook 1969–1970.
La Salle College Basketball Handbook 1970–1971.
La Salle Men's Basketball Media Guide 2016–2017.
La Salle University Basketball Yearbook 1989–1990.

Index

David Grzybowski is a former television news reporter for WPHL in Philadelphia, where he covered the 2015 visit by Pope Francis, the annual Philadelphia Mummers Parade, the 2016 Democratic National Convention, and the 2016 Villanova Wildcats NCAA championship run. He also reported for WNCN in Raleigh, North Carolina, where he covered both the 2017 University of North Carolina NCAA championship title run and Hurricane Matthew. Visit him online at tomgolabook.com.